WINFUEL

12 SECRETS TO NAVIGATING A WORLD WHERE WINNING IS JUST THE BEGINNING

DAN SOLOMON

ISBN (Paperback): 978-1962825665
ISBN (eBook): 978-1962825658

Published by **Atlas Elite Publishing**
www.atlaselitepublishingpartners.com

Powered by **Winfuel**
www.winfuel.com

Disclaimer

This book is intended for informational and educational purposes only. The author and publisher make no representations or warranties with respect to the accuracy or completeness of the contents and specifically disclaim any implied warranties of fitness for a particular purpose. The advice and strategies contained herein may not be suitable for every individual or situation. Readers should use their own judgment and, if necessary, consult a qualified professional before applying any of the ideas presented. The author and publisher shall not be held liable for any loss of profit or other damages arising directly or indirectly from the use of this book.

For information, inquiries, or permissions, please visit the publisher's website.

WINFUEL / noun /

A powerful source of energy and guidance aimed at
fueling sustainable growth and success.

TABLE OF CONTENTS

INTRODUCTION

This isn't a book about bodybuilding.

Yes it's true. I'm known mostly for a career in the business of muscle, an industry that measures in the billions. But this isn't a book about fitness, nor is it a life story. The lessons on these pages will take you much further than a self-indulgent memoir. That's another book for another day. This one is different. It isn't about building your body or losing weight. There are people more qualified than me to guide you through that process. Don't get me wrong, I love a good workout, that feeling we get when each painful rep sends blood directly into the muscle, a cure for the stresses of the day.

Let's face it, at the core of the fitness movement is a desire to transform, to maximize our potential, to become the best version of ourselves. But, like I said, you're not reading this to learn how to build a six pack. **You're reading it because you're business minded and you see something bigger,** an economy that's growing faster than any muscle you've ever trained and you've watched others turn their passions into financial security, and for some, generational wealth.

When I started writing this book, the target audience was the men and women who comprise the rapidly growing, global fitness community, the ones who reach out to me every day with dreams of turning their fit-focused lifestyle into a real career. But as I continued writing I realized quickly that the words on these pages can be applied to just about anyone who shares a *burning desire* to grow, to elevate, to capitalize on valuable relationships, maximizing opportunities and creating a life in business filled with good energy and sustainable success.

For many of you, you've already taken the leap. Your days are spent growing a company, building a brand, marketing a product, or creating strategic alliances. Your journey in the business of health, fitness, **or something entirely different** is already underway. And for the rest of you, you're in the exploratory phase, trying to identify the best point of entry, preparing to leverage your passion into something more valuable. Regardless of which category you fall into, you're not just looking to make a living. You're looking to achieve real success, the kind of success that changes everything.

The business of fitness has given me a lot, you'll hear about some of it on these pages. I've often called the fitness industry an entrepreneurial playground, loaded with ambition, a world ripe with opportunity. But this goes beyond fitness. It's for everyone.

The fact that you're reading this book sets you apart from many of your peers. Your thirst for insight and a competitive edge will take you a long way. Much like building your body, advancement and growth requires dedication, instincts, and a good plan.

The business of human performance continues to evolve. From nutrition and supplementation all the way to apparel, hormone therapy, event production, health clubs, equipment, functional foods, and media-- the opportunities are endless. Innovations in technology along with massive increases in participation have financial analysts forecasting significant increases in industry-wide revenue. As the world embraces anti-aging, longevity and the transformative powers of a fit lifestyle, there is no telling how high the ceiling will rise, but capitalizing on them requires a fundamental understanding of how to engage and adapt, positioning yourself for sustainable growth, separating yourself from the pack.

This isn't a "how to" manual or a roadmap. At its core, WINFUEL is a mindset. Some rules of engagement that should resonate across all industries. 12 secrets, each curated from decades in the high octane, competitive world of fitness, a rapidly growing economy that's showing no signs of slowing down. It's been said that the only true source of knowledge is the accumulation of experiences. I've had many.

A Word of My Own. Winfuel Defined.

WINFUEL / noun / A powerful source of energy and guidance aimed at fueling sustainable growth and success.

There's roughly 600,000 words in the Oxford English Dictionary, but I created a new one. Winfuel. It's a mindset and an approach. It's what powers the engine that drives purpose, influence and leadership. A core principle of WINFUEL is the notion that *winning is just the beginning*. While we all love to win, the most lucrative and meaningful conquests are often the ones that follow our initial triumphs.

On my personal journey toward the top of the fitness industry, I've made friends and I've made mistakes. I've had wins and losses, and I've learned from both. I've grown to understand the limitations of fear, the power of measuring risk, and the critical need to take ownership of my strengths and weaknesses. Humility is where growth begins. The 12 secrets on these pages have fueled countless wins, but more importantly, they've helped me connect and evolve, creating purpose in a world obsessed with short-sighted validation.

Those of you who follow my world will know that there have been 19 winners of the Mr. Olympia, the most coveted title in bodybuilding. While each of them have secured their place in history, not all of them got rich. Each of our iconic champions used their title and their status in different ways. Some of them, like Arnold Schwarzenegger, leveraged their status in ways that created success beyond measure. Arnold isn't alone. Other champions have turned their rise to the top into generational wealth. But not everyone had the instincts, or the playbook, to realize that winning is only the start of the journey. It's what you do with your wins, your relationships, and your opportunities that will ultimately write your story.

WINFUEL isn't just a collection of ideas. It's a mindset, an approach to winning that's larger than the win itself. My hope is that you'll connect with these ideas, grow from them, and allow yourself to leverage their effectiveness and their simplicity. The fuel to win.

A Little About Me:

To many of you, I'm the guy who runs the event widely regarded as the *Superbowl* of the fitness industry. The Mr. Olympia was created back in the mid 1960's by bodybuilding pioneer Joe Weider, a man who would later become a mentor to many of us who entered the world he created. Joe set the wheels in motion for an entire industry, long before there were gyms on every corner, before the arrival of the first supplement companies, back when Hollywood frowned upon muscle and sports teams hadn't started hiring team trainers. It was a different world when Joe started out, but he set out on a journey that started humbly with a subscription newsletter aimed at teaching people how to build their bodies. The newsletter eventually became a magazine. The magazine evolved into a publishing empire that he would later sell for a cool $350 million. Every sport has its mountain top, its highest achievement. Baseball has its World Series. In Football it's the Superbowl, Hockey has the Stanley Cup….and in the world of bodybuilding, it's the Olympia, the title that changes lives, builds legacies, and allows someone to be called *the best in the world.*

What started simply as the world championship of professional bodybuilding, "Olympia Weekend" would evolve into a global showcase of all things fitness, a bucket-list experience for men and women who come from around the world, a central artery of an entire industry. It would take several books to tell the story of Joe Weider, but let's suffice it to say that Joe didn't change the game, he created it. His life story was the subject of a movie that I Co-Produced in 2018 called BIGGER (Prime Video / Apple TV).

Joe passed away in 2013. My days are now spent advancing the work that he devoted his life to.

But let's back up a bit.

My journey in the business of fitness started long before I walked into a real gym for the first time. I first connected with a desire to be stronger when I was a kid. It wasn't a regular desire and it wasn't temporary. It was a burning desire, the kind that grabs a hold of you and won't let go. The transformative powers of a journey in fitness can serve as a path toward a different life. Mine started in the backyard of the first home I ever knew. The plates were rusty, the bar and the wobbly bench press weren't much, but it got the job done. The seed was planted.

A few months later, my dad and my older brother got into a big argument. I don't recall what it was about, but it was enough to make my dad leave the house to cool down for a few hours. When he returned, he handed me a membership card for a local gym. I'll never forget that night. He overcame the argument by visiting a nearby gym, a place he had never walked into, to buy me a membership. It was called Scandinavian Fitness. I'm not sure what came of it, but it was my first real gym and I had the membership card to prove it. My dad couldn't have possibly known at the time what he did for me that night.

I started reading the muscle magazines and books and anything that could provide a map to the treasure. In this case, the treasure wasn't anything I could buy. It had to be earned. I think that's what made it so appealing to me, a direct correlation between work, pain, consistency and results. I wanted to build my body because it was my chance to show my friends that I was willing to outwork them. From a young age, it was always my feeling that there was no greater reputation than to be known as someone willing to outwork everyone. Later in life I discovered that hard work was only a part of the formula.

In the fall of 1998, just a few years after I graduated college, I was in New York City on a weekend business trip. I was working as a financial planner for one of the big investment companies. It was my first full-time job. I never really enjoyed the job, but it paid the bills and I was pretty good at it. I used those years to learn my way around asset allocation, risk management, sales, and perhaps more valuable, I learned how to be a professional.

My hotel in New York that weekend was in Midtown Manhattan just up the street from the Paramount Theater, the famous auditorium located inside Madison Square Garden. In a twist of fate, the marquis outside the theater said "MR. OLYMPIA TONIGHT". Back in those days, before the arrival of social media, we didn't always know that something was happening in another city until we arrived. This was a great surprise!! I managed to get a ticket, a single seat, somewhere near the back of the theater. I had grown up following the famous bodybuilders and suddenly all the images from the pages of the magazines had come to life. I was blown away by it. I still remember the larger-than-life physiques on that stage. The roar of the crowd, the production, the drama on stage as the best in the world went pose for pose. When the show was over, I recall walking out of the theater that night, just a young man in his mid 20's. I remember thinking about the world I had just discovered. This wasn't just an event. It was an experience. My brain had been recalibrated. This was something I needed in my life. As I was trying to figure out what I was gonna do with my career, that night in New York became the ultimate plot twist.

Fast Forward: 20 years later. I found myself standing backstage at a sold-out Las Vegas arena, pacing nervously, awaiting my introduction. I walked out wearing a brand new suit, beneath the fitness industry's brightest lights, arrived at a podium, leaned into a microphone, and proudly welcomed nearly 10,000 fans to the biggest night in bodybuilding.

"Ladies & Gentlemen" I shouted, *"Welcome to the Olympia"*. I was now in charge.

While some might call that a victory lap, the truth is, my best moments have come when few others were watching. I love closing deals. Connecting with companies, new audiences, creators, and leaders. There's nothing more satisfying. I've raised more than 75 million dollars in an industry that many call "niche", and along the way I've helped others win. In chapter one you'll hear about *The Win-Win Equation*, an approach that has served me well. Later in the book you'll hear me talk about the fundamental importance of self awareness, seeing things through the eyes of the person you're negotiating with, exploring the idea that empathy isn't weakness, it's valuable data. We'll explore the power of a think tank and the role that fear plays on your road to the top. As you're reading my **12 Secrets to Navigating a World Where Winning is Just the Beginning** you'll discover that nearly everything in this book can be applied, tweaked or modified for anyone, in pursuit of anything. On the pages to follow you'll walk down a path that's as much about the *journey* as it is the destination. Because if you're holding this book, you may have already arrived.

The 12 Secrets

The Win-Win Equation

Prepare to be Misunderstood. It's Just Background Noise.

Fear is the Great Destroyer

Build Multi-Dimensional Value

Find the Humor

Self-Awareness is Everything

Don't Just Be an Idea Guy. Execute!!

Build a Think Tank

See it Through Their Eyes

Consistency is King

The Power of the Pivot

Train Your Mind to be Stronger Than Your Feelings

THE WIN-WIN EQUATION

"Every successful deal starts with choosing the long-term relationship over the short-term gain."

Warren Buffett

THE WIN-WIN EQUATION

The desire to win lives in all of us. It's a universal truth.

For most people, the concept of victory is a fairly basic idea. Someone wins, someone loses. That's the way we were taught to see competition, binary outcomes. But what if I told you that there's a far better way to define a winning deal?

And no, I'm not talking about the "Everyone's a Winner" participation trophy nonsense that gets handed out in youth sports leagues. I'm talking about real, meaningful, sustainable wins, the kind that come from building mutual value and trust. This is the essence of the WIN-WIN Equation.

The Harvard Law School Program on Negotiation defines a win-win negotiation as one in which both sides are satisfied with their agreement. It goes on to state that a win-win negotiation is the "ultimate goal in business negotiation," and when parties reach a win-win, "the odds of long-lasting success are much higher."

Understanding the WIN-WIN

A WIN-WIN isn't about soft negotiations or letting someone else take advantage of your goodwill. It's about creating outcomes where both parties gain real value and leave the table better than when they came. It's about designing partnerships that are not only beneficial now, but valuable long into the future.

In a world obsessed with domination and one-upmanship, this approach can seem counterintuitive. But in practice, it's what separates a short-lived transactional moment from something much bigger. Keep reading.

Rewriting the Rules of Negotiation

Too often, business negotiations feel like a boxing match. Two sides enter with their fists up, each one focused on taking as much as they can, revealing as little as possible, and definitely not showing vulnerability. The result? Disconnect, resentment, and deals that never reach their full potential.

This kind of thinking poisons possibility. It assumes that the other party is an obstacle rather than a potential partner. It's driven by fear…the fear of being outmaneuvered, undervalued, or taken advantage of.

But the best negotiators I know operate differently. They come to the table not just to win *for themselves*, but to help the other side win too. They don't view the process as a battle, but as an opportunity to **co-create value**. And when that happens, deals go from transactional to transformational.

Tapping Into the Theory of Abundance

At the heart of every true win-win outcome is a mindset, not just a tactic or a trick, but a core belief about how value is created and shared.

One of the most powerful principles in Stephen Covey's *7 Habits of Highly Effective People* is the **abundance mindset**. The belief that there is more than enough success, opportunity, and prosperity to go around. In a world wired to think in terms of scarcity, where winning means someone else has to lose, this concept is a game changer.

An abundance mindset reframes how we approach business, especially in high-stakes conversations and negotiations. Instead of seeing the pie as fixed and fearing that giving up a slice means you lose, you start to realize **the pie can grow.** In fact, with the right spirit of collaboration, the outcome can be bigger, better, and more beneficial for *everyone* involved.

That's the essence of a true win-win. When both parties walk away not with a divided prize, but with a multiplied one.

Involve the People Who See the Numbers and the Possibilities

One of the smartest things you can do when aiming for a win-win outcome? Bring your finance team into the room early. Here's why.

Finance professionals are wired to think in terms of total value: costs, outcomes, future returns, and strategic potential. While others may get caught up in surface-level trade-offs ("If I give them X, we lose Y"), your finance people can often identify opportunities for leverage, margin, growth, or alignment that might otherwise go unnoticed.

They help shift the focus from **what you're giving up** to **what you can gain together.** A truth that often lives in the math.

For example, you might balk at offering a client more favorable payment terms. But your CFO might recognize that those terms could unlock a longer contract, a more sustainable relationship or better cash flow timing…benefits that outweigh the initial concession.

Finance teams are not just bean counters, they're storytellers of value. They can help anchor your negotiation with a bigger picture view.

Reframe the Game

If you want to consistently create win-win deals, you have to let go of the "value extraction" mentality. Stop trying to take as much as possible from every interaction. Instead, approach negotiations with curiosity: What does success *really* look like for them? What are they not saying but clearly care about? What pain can I solve for them that costs me little but means everything to them?

This is where the real magic happens, when you solve problems the other party didn't even realize you could help with. That's not just negotiation. That's leadership.

And here's the kicker. When people feel understood, respected, and genuinely supported, they don't just agree to the deal…they become advocates. They tell others. They come back for more. And they look for ways to help *you* win next time.

That kind of reputation is priceless.

Lead with Value, Win with Trust

Win-Win isn't just a strategy. It's a philosophy of business and life.

It's about being generous, not naive. Strategic, not selfish. It's about playing the long game and recognizing that in a world of limited attention and infinite options, **those who help others win tend to win the most.**

So next time you walk into a negotiation, bring more than leverage. Bring vision. Bring empathy. Bring abundance.

Because when you do, you won't just walk out with a deal. You'll walk out with a partner and a platform for the next big win.

Dig Deeper

In sales, business development, and partnerships, a zero-sum mentality breeds conflict and often resentment. On the other hand, a WIN-WIN mindset fuels trust, ongoing opportunities, and deeper collaboration.

In my role as President of the Olympia, I've negotiated deals with major corporations, international partners, and startup founders. These sponsorships and alliances are highly coveted. Brands want to associate themselves with the prestige, the status, and the culture of the world's most celebrated fitness event brand.

But for me, the end goal isn't just to close the deal—it's to build a sustainable relationship. That means asking how I can make sure they win too. But it's not enough to just ask the question, it requires thoughtful and objective analysis, a sincere understanding of what their company needs to grow. Who's their target customer? What's the most effective way to deliver their message? How can my staff build in added value? And most importantly, what's the outcome that will create a high probability for continued business?

Creating win-win deals isn't about being soft. It's about being strategic, curious, and collaborative. Whether you're untangling opposing beliefs, navigating financial tradeoffs, or trying to future-proof an agreement, the key is shifting from "How do I win?" to "How do we both win?"

That mindset change is what turns deals into relationships, and transactions into long-term value.

Easier Said Than Done

In business negotiations, the "win-win" is the holy grail, an agreement where both sides walk away feeling they gained real value. But as any experienced negotiator knows, win-win outcomes aren't always easy to pull off.

Experts at Harvard Law School's Program on Negotiation have outlined powerful strategies to help even the toughest negotiations become collaborative, not combative.

When your proposal challenges the status quo, expect resistance. It's easy to assume the best move is to hit your counterpart with data proving how your idea serves the greater good. But that approach often backfires, coming off as one-sided and dismissive.

MIT professor Lawrence Susskind argues in his book **_Good for You, Great for Me_** that a better path is **joint fact-finding**. Rather than pushing your own version of the facts, invite both sides to explore the data together. This collaborative fact-gathering process helps build a shared foundation of truth before anyone digs into their positions.

The result? Reduced defensiveness, fewer assumptions, and a stronger basis for solutions.

One of the fastest ways to move toward a win-win is to **find common ground**. Instead of fighting over the same piece of the pie, look for ways to expand it, helping both sides envision new possibilities, making space for smarter, more creative agreements.

Real Examples from the Front Lines

Let's say I'm negotiating a multi-year sponsorship with a global supplement company. It's tempting to push for the biggest dollar amount possible, front-load the benefits on our side, and make the deal about what the Olympia gains.

…But that's a short-sighted strategy. What happens when the sponsor doesn't get the ROI they expected? What happens when they feel squeezed or undervalued?

Instead, I ask different questions: How will this sponsorship help their brand grow? What can we offer that makes this more than a logo on a backdrop? How can we create activations and content that allow their brand to genuinely connect with our audience?

When the sponsor feels like they're getting more than they asked for, when they *win* in real, measurable ways…that's when the partnership has staying power.

Reputation: The Long-Term Play

I view every partnership as a long-term investment. I don't want a one-night stand. I want a relationship. When both parties win, they *want* to keep working together. That leads to multi-year deals, deeper integration, and the kind of word-of-mouth that money can't buy.

In today's hyper-connected world, reputation is currency. Word travels fast. One lopsided deal, one short-sighted win, can tarnish your brand and your name. But when people know that you play fair, that you create value, and that you're invested in their success, they want to work with you. They recommend you. They come back.

Reputation isn't just about being liked. It's about being trusted. And the WIN-WIN equation is the foundation of that trust.

The Obligatory Baseball Analogy

If you and I both run Major League Baseball teams and we decide to trade players, a successful trade means that *both* teams get better. If I "rob" you in the trade, you'll think twice before ever doing business with me again. Needless to say, the objective is always to create a competitive advantage for your team, but when the deal is finalized you should be rooting for the player you traded as much as you root for the player you received.

A one-sided victory might stroke your ego in the moment, but it could close a door. And in business, closed doors often cost you more than what you've gained in a one-time win.

The Map to the WIN-WIN

1. **Start with Empathy**: Understand what the other party truly values. Not just the surface-level needs, but the deeper motivators.
2. **Communicate Transparently**: Lay everything out. Hidden agendas and half-truths are the quickest way to destroy trust.
3. **Create Value Beyond the Deal**: What else can you offer that they weren't expecting? Surprise them in a good way.
4. **Play the Long Game**: Don't maximize short-term profit at the expense of long-term success.
5. **Follow Through**: Do what you say you're going to do. Be reliable. Be consistent.

It's Not About Being Soft—It's About Being Strategic

A WIN-WIN approach isn't weakness. It's strength with a broader vision. It requires discipline, creativity, and emotional intelligence. It often means having the courage to give before you receive, knowing that the return will come.

The most respected dealmakers I know don't gloat. They don't high-five when they squeeze a partner. They smile quietly, knowing they created something lasting.

Shift from me to WE, listen first speak second, find the overlap, guard the relationship and play the long game. And let's be real…this approach doesn't guarantee you won't get burned. There will be times when someone takes advantage of your generosity. That's part of the game. But over the long haul, WIN-WIN thinkers outperform. They build bigger networks. They rise to the top of their industry.

It's Not What You Get. It's What You Build

At the end of the day, creating win-win relationships is about playing a bigger game. It's not just about what you get, it's about what you build. When you align your goals with the goals of others, everyone becomes invested in your success. And when that happens, you're no longer just chasing opportunities…you're creating them. Together.

If winning is your only goal, your ceiling will always be lower. But if *winning together* is your aim, the possibilities are endless. Think bigger. Give more. Build relationships that last. That's where the real WINFUEL comes from.

Because in this world, where everyone is chasing victory, the smartest play isn't winning once. It's winning again and again.

That's the WIN-WIN equation.

PREPARE TO BE MISUNDERSTOOD. IT'S JUST BACKGROUND NOISE.

"To Be Great is to be Misunderstood."

Ralph Waldo Emerson

PREPARE TO BE MISUNDERSTOOD.
IT'S JUST BACKGROUND NOISE.

Background Noise. Some call it static. Others use the term to describe outside elements or opinions that disrupt momentum, focus or productivity. Background noise comes in all shapes and sizes, but at its core, it's the enemy of progress.

Identifying background noise is the easy part. But reducing it is considerably more challenging.

Background noise is everywhere, so don't build a plan to eliminate it. That's like trying to eliminate all the misinformation on social media, a battle you won't win. The secret to reducing background noise lies within how you choose to process the noise.

Your plans are big. Your ideas are bold. Not everyone will understand. So prepare to be misunderstood.

Everyone has an opinion, a vantage point born from their own life experiences, and their own limitations. Not everyone has the ability or the desire to see your vision. Learn to understand the difference between constructive feedback and empty rhetoric, commonly known as hot air. Abandon your need for approval. Someone once told me that the secret to prolonging positive momentum is to be selective with who you share it with.

Background noise is even louder when you're in a business of mass consumption. **What's mass consumption?** Simply put, it means a lot of people are watching what you do. As president of the Olympia, I oversee an event that means so much to so many. Scrutiny is intense. Millions watch closely as I make decisions that impact a world they devote their lives to. Pleasing everyone is impossible. My productivity increased 10X the moment I began to understand the absurdity of trying to make everyone happy.

Conviction will take you a long way. Before you begin, take ownership of the reality that your ideas won't be universally loved. Don't live in fear of your critics, be empowered by them. Find inspiration in knowing that they're watching closely, find freedom in knowing that there's no pathway to making everyone happy. I'll say it again. Find FREEDOM in the reality that you will NEVER make everyone happy. Stick to your plan, your vision and your path. Let them talk, while you grow. Let them criticize, while you build.

Conviction Over Consensus

When you tune in to the background noise, you pay a price. You lose time. You lose focus. You may even lose faith in yourself. Momentum is fragile. It takes so much effort to build and so little to destroy. One negative comment can spiral into days or weeks of paralysis. A little noise can make you question a vision you've carried for years.

And the worst part? Most people don't even realize they've surrendered. They wake up years later and wonder where their fire went. Or even worse, they'll discover that someone else, with more conviction and more courage, took their idea to the finish line.

Innovation doesn't come from consensus, it comes from conviction. Every disruptor, pioneer, or visionary was told they were doing it wrong.

So why do we listen in the first place?

It's human nature to seek belonging, safety, approval, and certainty. Historically, survival meant staying with the tribe and following the group. In today's world, that instinct translates to avoiding criticism, rejection, or failure. Make sense?

The road to the top, however, often demands that we **break away**. To create something extraordinary, you often have to go alone, or at least be willing to stand apart. That can be scary. The background noise offers a way back to safety. It tempts you with comfort and conformity. It says, "Stay small. Don't make waves. Don't be seen."

But safety is not the same as success. And comfort is the enemy of growth.

To manage background noise, it's important to first understand the various sources of the noise:

1. The Well-Meaning Worrier: This is the person who genuinely cares about you. It might be a parent, a spouse, a colleague, or a best friend. They want to protect you from disappointment and failure, so they try to nudge you toward safer ground.

2. The Realist: This is the person who prides themselves on seeing the world as it is. They believe they're doing you a favor by lowering your expectations. They see ambition as delusion and risk as recklessness. They confuse real vision with fantasy.

3. The Projectionist: They see your boldness as a reminder of what they didn't pursue. Your drive exposes their own inaction. Instead of dealing with that pain, they project it onto you. They'll say, "I tried something like that once; it didn't work."

4. The Distracted Masses: Social media, trending opinions, and the 24/7 news cycle create a chorus of noise. They clutter your mental space, and they try their hardest to distort your priorities.

5. Your Own Inner Voice: Perhaps the most dangerous of all the noise is the one that lives inside your head. It recycles every negative comment you've ever heard and delivers it in your own voice.

The Visionary's Burden

It's a term we hear a lot. **Visionary**. Someone who merges boldness, creativity and courage to see possibilities before others do. Visionaries are judged, criticized and wildly misunderstood. And while we all love a good label, the attributes that determine whether you're a true visionary need to be examined before we can proceed. Here's a few of them:

Imaginative – Can you see beyond your world, and encourage others to dream along with you? Are you constantly looking for ways to fix things, craft things, change things to be better? If you answered yes to these questions, then it's likely you're a visionary.

Persistent – A Visionary understands that winning isn't easy. They navigate challenges and even take a few punches, adjusting and pivoting. A visionary is at their best when the noise is at its loudest. Fully prepared to be misunderstood.

Courageous – Visionaries encourage their teams to fail fast, as long as they adapt and grow along the way. Visionaries take calculated risks, they don't fear the failure, they fear regret. The kind of regret that comes from not going all-in.

Optimism – A visionary doesn't take things personally and they're not easily offended. Their skin is thick. They radiate a different kind of energy, seeing the win long before it comes. It's a matter of "when"…..not "if".

Abandon your need for approval. The Only One Who Needs to Believe is YOU.

Protect Your Momentum

Momentum is the driver of progress. When you're in the zone, even small actions create a sense of flow, confidence, and clarity. But background noise interrupts that. It creates friction. You start second-guessing. You hesitate. You wait for permission or approval, the kind that may never come……and here's what happens next:

- You start researching more instead of building.
- You seek validation before taking the next step.
- You spend more time planning than executing.
- You abandon the plan at the first sign of criticism.

When you start spending valuable time defending your plan rather than executing it, you've already given the background noise more power than it deserves. If you had been fully *prepared to be misunderstood*, you wouldn't have given that power away.

The Myth of Consensus

One of the biggest traps is trying to get everyone on board. Consensus is not a prerequisite for progress. In fact, if everyone agrees with you early on, your idea is probably too safe, too familiar, or too small. So be careful what you ask for. Learn to embrace disagreement. Learn to stand alone if necessary. **Affirm your vision daily.** Write it down. Speak it. Visualize it. The more you affirm your purpose, the less you'll be affected by the noise.

- **J.K. Rowling** was rejected by twelve publishers before Harry Potter was published.
- **Walt Disney** was told he lacked imagination.
- **Oprah Winfrey** was told she was unfit for television.
- **Elon Musk** was laughed at for many of his ideas, including space travel.

They succeeded not because they had unanimous support but because they refused to let noise become truth and they were prepared to be misunderstood.

The Role of Self-Talk

Your inner monologue is the most persistent sound you'll ever hear. If it echoes the voices of the doubters, your actions will reflect hesitation. If it echoes your belief in yourself, your actions will reflect courage. This isn't about arrogance or ignoring feedback. It's about protecting your vision, guarding your mental environment.

Your Vision, Your Responsibility

No one will care about your plan as much as you do. That's not a flaw in the system, that's just how it works. It's *your* job to build belief, it's not *their* job to fully understand it, especially in the beginning. Prepare yourself to be misunderstood. It's part of the equation. Don't become dependent on validation. Trust the process. Don't wait for anyone else to provide you with the fuel to win. You already have it.

FEAR IS THE GREAT DESTROYER

"

"Everything you've ever wanted is sitting on the other side of fear."

George Addair

FEAR IS THE GREAT DESTROYER

It's the silent assassin. It kills innovation, limits growth, and stops progress dead in its tracks. Before we go too far down this road, let's first try to better understand how fear works.

It's a complex human emotion. Fear is designed to protect us from reckless choices, serving as an internal alarm to help keep us away from danger. Fear can be your friend, a mechanism of the brain designed to keep us out of harm's way. But like many things that are designed to help us, there's another side to fear, a far less positive side.

Fear holds us back from trying things, from experimenting, from testing boundaries. Fear is an emotion that literally prevents us from doing the things that **need to be done** in order to grow. In order to dominate.

So how is it possible that something so helpful can also be so destructive?

To put it simply, it's all about **control**. The average person allows fear to control them, while the world's true achievers and industry leaders have the ability to control how they utilize and manage the effects of fear.

Full disclosure

No one is *fearless*. That's a word we hear a lot, but no one is truly without fear. I'm afraid of many things (and so are you). I'm not a fan of rollercoasters and you won't see me skydiving anytime soon. But when it comes to business, I've learned to understand the amazing things that can happen when we leave our comfort zone, converting fear from a detriment into a powerful source of Winfuel.

Comfort: The Enemy of Progress

Start by embracing discomfort. Understand that the uneasy feeling in your stomach is part of the growth process. The *unknown* isn't the enemy, it's the pathway to everything you've always wanted. Understand the power of momentum, reminding yourself that momentum grows with each step you take. When you take those first steps, your focus begins to shift from fear to movement, taking you further and further from the fear that once held you back.

The unknown isn't the enemy, it's the portal.

Knowing Your Value

You might be wondering, what does *knowing your value* have to do with the idea of fear? Well here's the deal. In business, it's fear that keeps us from asking for more. Whether it's money, better opportunities, or more value, fear is often the thing that holds us back from negotiating the best possible deal.

Sometimes we view "asking for more" as imposing or risky. But when you truly know your value, or the value of what you're giving, the dynamic begins to shift. You'll suddenly feel the freedom to ask for what you deserve and what's appropriate. When you don't know your value, you shrink, you accept less. And let's be clear about something, knowing your value is NOT arrogance. It's a form of self-respect, the kind that prevents fear from weakening your position.

Before we dig deeper, here's a few simple steps to help you gain control:

1. **Acknowledge the Feeling**

   Identify the specific fear. Name it. Own it.

2. **Risk/Reward Analysis**

   What are you risking in a worst-case scenario *and* what does a win look like?

3. **Break It into Steps**

   Large unknowns can paralyze you. Take one manageable step forward. Then another. Momentum builds.

4. **Use the Fear**

   Channel adrenaline into clarity. Remind yourself that what you're feeling is born from passion. Fear is just a word that turns it negative.

Fear of Losing

One of the most debilitating human emotions is the fear of losing and the fear of loss. In business, we spend endless amounts of energy in fear of losing a deal, or a job, or an important client. Society has created a definition for success that's built around status, money and possessions. Fear of losing those things can lead you down a path of self-preservation, **the avoidance of risk**. Some call this "playing small", holding back to avoid rejection or public scrutiny. When you add it all up, valuable opportunities are lost. The sooner you fully understand that losses are part of the road to the top, the easier this becomes.

A Deeper Dive

Understanding the difference between those who shrink and those who explode requires a fear analysis. The things that scare you the most are the things that are holding you back. Look at what you fear, really look at it. Are you afraid of failure? Rejection? Judgment?

When you break it down, fear is simply a reflection of the things you've built walls around. Identifying the fear shows you exactly where you're limiting your potential, where you're playing small.

Ask yourself, what would happen if you stopped letting fear make your decisions for you? What if, instead of backing away every time fear shows up, you leaned into it? Fear is pointing you to the exact areas in your life that need your attention.

It's revealing the limits you've set for yourself, limits that are often self-imposed. When you face your fears, you start to break down those limits, and that's where growth begins.

Here's the thing, your brain will always over-value loss. It magnifies what might go wrong and minimizes what could go right. Most people overestimate loss and underestimate gain when evaluating decisions. A big part of overcoming fear is inverting that dynamic.

The Marshmallow Challenge

Tom Wujec, a Canadian tech visionary, once gave a TED Talk where he shared a story about something he called "The Marshmallow Challenge".

He explained how he performed this challenge with CEOs, Engineers, Business School Graduates, Kindergarteners, and Architects. Teams of four were each given a marshmallow along with 20 sticks of spaghetti, some tape and some string.

Each group was given 18 minutes to build the tallest tower possible. The only requirement was that the marshmallow had to be at the top of their tower. The tallest tower would win the competition.

As it turned out, some of the top performers were the kindergarteners. The worst performers were the recent graduates of business school.

Wait, what? How did the kindergarteners, with their one year of education, do better than the business school graduates?

Well, here's what happened.

The college graduates spent the entire time carefully designing their structure. At the last minute, just before their time expired, they tried to stand it up. Once lifted, their tower crumbled under the surprising weight of the marshmallow. Who knew a marshmallow was so heavy?

Oh wait, the kindergartners knew. They learned it by erecting their structure quickly & fearlessly and watching it collapse **long before the 18 minutes were up**. In fact, they tried to stand their building up several times before they finally got it right. **Since they weren't afraid to fail**, they learned immediately that the heavy marshmallow would create challenges in getting their tower to balance. Their ability to learn that lesson early in their 18 minute allotment gave them all the time they needed to make the necessary adjustments. Make sense?

The Public Speaking Dilemma

Nearly every list of "Most Feared Things in Business" places public speaking near the top. There's something about speaking, in a room filled with people, that triggers the body to react. The heart speeds up, palms get sweaty, anxiety threatens to take over.

But here's the deal, **this fear MUST be dealt with**.

Why? Because being a leader, building influence, and growing companies requires a fundamental ability to communicate and connect. It's a responsibility. It's part of the gig. My apologies for the tough love, but there is nothing optional about it.

I stand on stages around the world connecting with those who aspire to maximize their genetic potential, delivering words that are wrapped around the transformational message of the fitness lifestyle. People often ask me how I became good at it. The truth is, I didn't always enjoy it. When I was in highschool I joined the debate team and started developing a baseline ability to communicate. But that's NOT what made me a good public speaker. Those debates scared the shit out of me.

I'll tell you when I went from "giving speeches" to being someone who can command a room, a theater, or an arena. It all happened with one game-changing revelation. Follow closely.

The moment I allowed myself to fully understand that my words carried weight, that people wanted to hear what I had to say, **that's when everything changed**. The fear faded, the anxiety disappeared. My previous mindset always led me down a path where I felt like the audience was judging me. Until I realized that my words were providing real value. I was educating. Providing clarity. Giving cautionary advice. I was no longer doing it for me, I was now doing it for THEM and they wanted to hear it. In many cases, they NEEDED to hear it. That mindset changed everything.

The moment you realize your words have the power to inspire, assist and elevate, suddenly your focus shifts from fear to purpose. Before you walk on stage or before you begin your presentation, tell yourself that you have nothing to prove. No one is there to judge you. They are there because they genuinely seek what you have to share. There is no better way to change the way you feel about public speaking than to understand that you are giving, not taking.

There are countless books and courses out there aimed at helping you become an elite public speaker, but my advice on the subject is simple:

Embrace the idea that what you have to say needs to be heard. Take ownership of the reality that your words are the seeds to grow a movement, or build a company, or create influence. The only thing scarier than talking to a room full of strangers is the tragedy of wasting valuable opportunities to impact the lives of those who need to hear what you have to say.

Take Your Shot

Winning starts with a belief, a conviction. Taking your shot isn't simply about an outcome, it's about having a belief – in yourself!! Whether it's a multi-million dollar deal, a major acquisition, or something smaller, whether it's in public or private, TAKE YOUR SHOT. Don't wait for perfect timing. No more second guessing.

Every success story comes down to a few moments, a crossroad that can forever change the course of history. Your history, your story. It was Wayne Gretzky who famously said "You miss 100% of the shots you don't take."

And remember – Courage isn't the absence of fear, it's the ability to make progress in spite of it.

BUILD
MULTI-DIMENSIONAL
VALUE

"

"Skill stacking is the ultimate unfair advantage"

Sahil Bloom

BUILD MULTI-DIMENSIONAL VALUE

If you've gotten to know me over the years, you already know that baseball has always been a part of my life. It's one of the things that connected me to my father and it's built an even stronger bond between me and my son. Some think the game is boring, but for me it's a work of art, blending strategy with skill, failure and redemption.

One of the endearing parts of the game is evaluating the players, tracking their stats, and monitoring their performance. Each player is unique. Some are known for their ability to power the ball over the fence, while others have reputations for their exceptional arm strength, speed, or their elite defense.

But every once in a while a player comes along who can perform in all parts of the game, the rarest of talents. These are **the unicorns.**

In baseball, we call them "5-Tool Players", that special breed who can do just about everything – with their bat, their power, their arm, their glove, and their legs – the total package!!!

In business, multi-dimensional competency is the *holy grail* and it's rarer than you might think. I've spent years developing an ability to perform all phases of a deal cycle; From building the framework of a partnership…to presenting it…to closing the deal, raising capital when needed, writing the press release, promoting it, and executing the elements of a successful long-term partnership.

Turn Yourself into a Solution

Just like investing, skills compound. The more you learn, the more you're able to do…and the bigger your wins get.

Let's say you're a strong communicator. Great. But if you can also build the pitch deck, assess the market, negotiate the contract, and follow up with marketing? Now you're not just a salesperson—you're a solution. You're not just an executive—you're an asset. You're not just an entrepreneur—you're a powerhouse, a UNICORN.

Your job is not just to be good at the thing you're working on. Your job is to be able to directly influence the overall vision and all the verticals that comprise it.

But What About Just Mastering One Thing?

For decades, we were taught to pick a lane and master it. And yes, there's real value in expertise. But in today's rapidly shifting economy, *range* is the new flex. The individuals and leaders who thrive in the current climate are those who can think like strategists, communicate like marketers, execute like operators, and build like engineers. They are adaptable, agile, and highly valuable because they deliver **multi-dimensional value**.

You don't have to be elite at everything. But you do have to bring more than just one thing to the table. Your depth of contribution becomes a competitive advantage when you not only **see the big picture**, but also **act on the details**.

Despite the allure of a specialized skill, the world's most intriguing people have always been *polymaths*, dynamic performers with a broader understanding across multiple disciplines.

And look, I get it. We were taught to be experts at one thing. From the time we entered school we were encouraged to specialize, to choose a path and stick with it. Niche expertise can be profitable. Lawyers, doctors, engineers, and investment bankers are well paid for their knowledge. After all, no one wants someone who dabbles in medicine to remove their gallbladder. But in the world of business, especially for those reading this book, a narrow skillset seldom garners attention, or opportunity.

Breaking Down Multi-Dimensional Value

Before you get dizzy trying to understand how to re-brand yourself as a multifaceted power player, let's take a look at what multi-dimension really looks like:

1. **Strategic Thinking** – The ability to see patterns, identify leverage points, and map the game plan.
2. **Execution** – Taking ideas from vision to reality without constant oversight.
3. **Influence and Communication** – Knowing how to shape narratives, pitch ideas, inspire audiences, and align people.
4. **Emotional Intelligence** – Navigating relationships, feedback, pressure, cultural differences, and uncertainty…with poise.
5. **Leadership Through Action** – Inspiring others through example, energy, and purpose.

A diversified skill stack isn't just practical—it's magnetic. It allows you to move across roles, industries, and audiences with power. The most valuable people I know are "skill stackers". They collect capabilities from different disciplines and experiences, *recombining them* in ways that create something rare. They're the marketer who also understands how to analyze data. The developer who can lead a team. The founder who can also design. These aren't just unicorns, they're *learners.*

Build Range Without Losing Focus

Now, let's be clear: Multi-dimensional doesn't mean distracted. It's about building range with intention. The goal is not to do everything. It's to understand enough of the system to navigate, lead, and provide value across it.

Think of it like this:

- **Specialists** perform in their lane.
- **Generalists** connect broader ideas across different domains.
- **Multi-dimensional players** do both, they perform in their lanes and they build intersections to bring it all together.

This is how you become the connective tissue in your organization, your industry, your network. Be the guy who understands how the dots connect, show them that you're able to see beyond the deal, beyond the decision, and beyond the moment.

Begin By Honestly Assessing Your Value

Take inventory:

- What are your top 2–3 core competencies?
- Where are your biggest blind spots?
- What skill, if mastered, would take you to an entirely new level?
- What's one adjacent capability you could build this year?

Building value isn't something you do in a single sprint. It's a lifestyle, a *refusal to be one-dimensional.*

The Shaq Effect.

Value is more than what you do. It's what you share.

Over the years, I've had some remarkable people in my life. Please forgive the name drop, but one of them is Shaquille O'Neal, a good friend, and one of the most recognizable celebs on the planet. Since his days dominating the NBA, Shaq has proven to be a formidable businessman, building a portfolio that may soon reach a billion-dollar valuation.

Shaq is different than most of my famous friends.

There are several ways to define the idea of generosity. For some, generosity is measured simply by how willing someone is to contribute financially. But there's a different kind of generosity that few ever talk about. The willingness to **share** key relationships and valuable wisdom. That kind of generosity is rare.

He always wants to help. There have been times when Shaq will ask me if I'm currently doing business with someone in particular, typically referring to a major company or TV network. The minute he discovers I haven't yet formed a relationship with that company, he pulls out his phone, dials the number, and puts me on a call with the CEO. His network is massive, some of the biggest companies in the world. Shaq likes to share.

He doesn't do it because he has to. He does it because he genuinely wants others to succeed. Most in his position prefer to guard their relationships, as opposed to sharing them. But Shaq is different. He's generous with his network, routinely bringing well-intentioned individuals together. He does this because he has created his own brand of generosity and he understands that sometimes money isn't nearly as valuable as sharing things that can help someone grow in a more meaningful way. He has succeeded in just about everything he's tried. From basketball to entertainment to production to law enforcement to business, the list goes on. But what truly separates him is his willingness to open doors for others, not just himself. He understands that shared opportunity has a way of multiplying itself. – The moral of this story: Generosity is a skill and an identity. It doesn't go unnoticed. Be generous with your value. Bring people together. Give them the tools to win. Because in the end, your value isn't just in what you do, it's in what you leave behind.

Final Thought

The best people I've done business with weren't just performers, they were **multipliers.** They could walk into a room and elevate the game. They weren't defined by their accolades, they were defined by their impact, by their multi-dimensional value.

Be that person. The one who delivers more than they expected. Don't just be the one they want, be the one they **need**.

FIND THE HUMOR

"Laughter is the shortest distance between two people."

Victor Borge

FIND THE HUMOR

Business isn't always fun.

Some days are ruthless, a relentless game of maneuvering, strategy, and emotion. It's unpredictable, high-stakes, and sometimes messy. We try our best to separate our business lives from our personal lives, but the wear and tear crosses over. It shows up in our bodies, our tone, our sleep, our energy, and even our spirit.

It's easy to get caught up in the seriousness of it all, scaling a company, closing deals, building an audience, meeting quotas, raising capital, protecting a brand. But here's the hard truth:

If you don't learn how to create levity in a tough negotiation, or in nearly any business scenario, you'll risk escalating tension, potentially closing the door to heightened creativity, powerful connection, and valuable collaboration.

The Levity Effect

There's a common misconception that humor and high performance don't mix. That levity and leadership are mutually exclusive. Some will tell you that if you're laughing, you're not serious about the objectives.

The truth is, laughter is **fuel**. Humor is strategy. And if used properly, it's one of the most powerful and multifaceted leadership and dealmaking tools in your arsenal.

Humor defuses tension, builds trust and humanizes your message. It builds connection and opens the door to so much more.

This isn't just an arbitrary theory. The science backs it up. Research from Stanford and Harvard shows that humor increases status and perceived intelligence, when it's used appropriately. In other words, if you make someone laugh and they *respect you for it*, they'll not only like you more, but they'll remember you longer. Both are vital pathways to building trust.

The Psychology of Humor

There's a reason you remember that one speaker from a conference five years ago, but forgot half the spreadsheets you saw this week.

Humor engages more parts of the brain. It lights up the **prefrontal cortex**, associated with higher-level thinking, while also triggering **dopamine**, the pleasure chemical that helps encode memories. This means when people laugh with you, they're also *remembering you*.

Want to increase audience retention or engagement in a presentation? Open with a relatable (and humorous) story.

Want to shift the energy in a tense room? Loosen things up with some self-deprecation.

Humor is *glue*. It makes your message stick. And it sends a message that you don't take yourself too seriously.

Humor Signals Confidence, Not Clownery

The right kind of humor in business signals leadership and authority. It shows you're secure enough to laugh. That you're not fragile. That your skin is thick and you can roll with the punches. Humor builds relatability.

This is particularly effective with your team. When you're able to laugh in tough times, not in denial, but in *defiance*, you model resilience. You show them that pressure doesn't have to kill the fun.

And when people associate *you* with joy, they want to be around you. They want to work with you. They want to do business with you.

You Don't Have to Be Funny to Use Humor

Now let's be clear about something. I'm NOT telling you to become a stand-up comedian. Sorry to break it to you, but most of us aren't that funny.

Sometimes it can be as simple as:

- Laughing about a past failure that taught you something.
- Telling a story about a recent screw-up, something relatable.
- Noticing how your Zoom shirt doesn't match the pajama pants they can't see.

You don't even need to be "funny" to *find* humor. You don't need punchlines to create lightness. You just need to be willing to see the absurdity, the irony, and the chaos of real life, and be okay letting others in on it. Humor is human and if used correctly, it can build lucrative energy and connection.

The Art of Self-Deprecation

Here's where things get interesting. Self-deprecation, when used with *confidence*, can create instant connection.

Why? Because it disarms people. It says, "Hey, I'm not perfect either."

Leaders and power-players are often put on pedestals, so the one who can lighten the mood by acknowledging that they have *the perfect face for radio* is often the one who earns trust. Here's what it does:

- It reduces the pressure in the room.
- It creates permission for others to open up, without fear.
- It makes people root for you, not resent you. A game changer.

Caution: There's a line. Self-deprecating humor should be strategic, NOT self-sabotaging. You're poking fun at yourself *because* you're secure, not because you need validation. You're still a force of nature. But you're human and you're not afraid to be vulnerable.

The message is simple: "I take my work seriously, but not myself."

Understanding Cultural Intelligence

Humor in business comes with a degree of risk. What's funny to you may not land the same way with someone from a different culture, generation, or background. Know your audience!!!

Cultural Intelligence is the ability to effectively connect and relate across other cultures, understanding values and accepted behavior. For example, in certain Middle-Eastern cultures, self-deprecating humor can be seen as weakness or even incompetence. It can also be viewed as disloyal if the humor groups in other members of your team.

The most successful people I know are culturally intelligent. They know when to lean in and when to hold back. They understand the delicate balance between levity and respect.

Some safe bets for business humor that keep you out of trouble:

- Observational humor (about shared experiences)
- Relatable frustrations (airport delays, tech glitches, etc)

When in doubt, read the room. Humor should lift, not divide. Sometimes humor can be rooted in self-awareness, as opposed to self-deprecation. It's an intuitive process.

Humor as a Company Builder

Let's take a moment and look at this through a leadership lens.

Some of the most influential leaders in the world have mastered the art of leading with heart as well as levity.

Sara Blakely, founder of Spanx, famously shares stories of her early rejections and wardrobe malfunctions to help her team feel safe taking risks. She's learned the power of turning embarrassing experiences, from her past, to engaging and relatable moments. But she doesn't stop there. She created something called "Oops Meetings" at her company where her team is encouraged to openly share their "screw-ups" and embarrassing rejections with the rest of the team. Her use of humor and humility helped turn her brand into a billion-dollar empire, without losing its soul.

It's simple. If you want someone to open up and fully engage… let them laugh *with* you. Show them that behind the numbers, the wins, the losses and the accolades, there's a human being, a pulse.

Bottom line? People do their best work when they feel good.

When organizations create room for laughter, they:

- Reduce turnover
- Improve morale
- Increase productivity
- Foster innovation & creative energy

Bringing it Down to Earth

Have you ever heard someone describe a memorable encounter with someone they've always admired? Like the time they met a famous athlete, or a movie star, or even a billionaire business mogul. If the encounter was a positive one, you'll often hear them say something like, "He was so down to earth!!!".

But what is it that makes a person come across as **down to earth** when they're driving a Bentley and living in a Palm Beach mansion? Most of the time, it's a dose of self-deprecation. A fun, relatable story to lighten the moment.

In a world filled with egos, bravado and assholes, there's something magnetic about those who are secure enough to merge humility and humor in a way that builds connection.

In my role as President of the Olympia, I'll often meet men and women who closely follow the world of bodybuilding and fitness. Many of them have dreams of reaching the Olympia stage or one day checking off a bucket-list item by attending the event. They grew up idolizing our champions and, in that brief encounter with me, they feel a connection to a world that means so much to them. Often times, I can see in their eyes that they're nervous, maybe even a bit stressed about saying the right thing or asking the right question. In these situations I'll almost always try to lighten the mood, reminding them that we're all in this together. It doesn't have to be a joke to be funny. Sometimes it's just a fun, light-hearted story about the "craziness" of building our bodies or the insanity of "suffering" the way we do to reach our goals. Suddenly, their eyes change from nervous to excited and their focus shifts from asking awkward questions to having a real conversation, exchanging real ideas.

Humor Does What Logic Can't

We've all been in negotiations where the data was right, the terms were fair, but the deal fell through. Why?

Because people don't always respond to numbers and logic. They respond to *feeling*.

Well intentioned humor can create a feeling. A connection.

Believe it or not, some deals get done simply because they *liked* you. Because they connected with you. Because for a moment, it didn't feel like business, it felt like a conversation between people who trust each other, the kind of trust that can be the bridge to so much more. In a sea of data, analysis, and accounting, it's often the human side that signals the instinct to proceed.

A few tips, if you need help

Here's how you start turning humor into real strategy:

- **Notice the funny** – Start journaling small moments that made you laugh. Make good use of them.
- **Practice light storytelling** – Try opening meetings with a quick story that reveals your human side.
- **Embrace your quirks** – Stop hiding your awkwardness. Own it. It's endearing.

- **Lead with lightness** – Before a tough conversation or pitch, ask yourself: *"How can I bring some warmth into this moment?"*

The Last Laugh

You don't need to choose between being effective and being funny. True power is in the ability to do both. Humor is more than a release, it's a **resource**, because in business, laughter won't just make you feel better. It'll make you a better leader, a better negotiator, a better closer.

So the next time you're navigating your most intense opportunities, remember one important thing. Sometimes the Winfuel lies in how human you're willing to be.

SELF-AWARENESS IS EVERYTHING

"Knowing yourself is the beginning of all wisdom."

Aristotle

SELF-AWARENESS IS EVERYTHING

It's been said that one of the biggest differences between animals and humans is the capacity to be self-aware, to understand our own strengths, weaknesses and vulnerabilities. Small dogs, for example, don't usually know they're small (and easily breakable) often leading to a tragic ending.

For humans, self-awareness is nearly as important as food and water. Without it, you're fucked. If you don't know who you are, what you're made of, how you're wired, or what you're bad at, you'll spend your life chasing shadows, reacting instead of creating, apologizing instead of dominating.

The stakes are high. Self-awareness, in many ways, is the survival tool of our species. It determines whether we evolve or stagnate, whether we align or fracture, whether we win or lose.

Self-awareness teaches us how to manage ourselves and how to productively engage with other people with a keen understanding of how they see us. You can't lead if you're unaware of how you're perceived.

Let's Start with General Awareness

In its most basic form, "awareness" is what you notice in life. It's about paying attention.

It's the details you pick up from your interaction with the world. It's your consciousness actively gathering and processing information from your environment. It's how you experience life. There's lots of things to notice each day, each hour, each moment. Look around right now and scan the area around you. What did you notice? Which details can you describe?

Are you aware of other people? Do you pick up on their vibe or energy? Do you notice how people interact with each other in a group? Do you notice physical details and movements of people, even strangers. At the heart of it all is the idea of being curious and brutally honest about what's in front of you. But true dominance begins with your ability to shine that level of awareness on yourself.

Self-Analysis and the Courage to Own It

Self-awareness exists on multiple levels. At the most basic level, it's physical. Understanding your body's strengths and weaknesses. This is instinctual and often life-preserving. Are you a fast runner? Do you have good endurance? Can you swim in deep water? But the more powerful…and elusive…forms of self-awareness are mental, intellectual, and emotional.

To be truly self-aware is to know where you excel and where you fall short. It means confronting the inconvenient truths about your behavior, not just your abilities. Do you take criticism well, or just pretend to? Do you communicate well? Do you adapt to stress or let it break you down? Do you come across trustworthy and authentic?

Are you well-liked? These aren't easy questions, but having the courage to ask them, and answer them, is the difference between living a life of impact or one of delusion.

If "awareness" is about tuning into the world around you, then "self-awareness" is the art of turning that lens inward. It's your ability to observe your own emotions, reactions, habits, behaviors, and thought patterns…as if you're watching yourself from the outside. It's like becoming both the star of the movie and the audience, all at the same time.

Think of it as tapping into your inner compass: your intuition, your gut feeling, your sixth sense. It's that quiet voice beneath the noise that knows when something feels off, even if everything looks fine on the surface. Self-awareness is really just radical honesty with yourself.

We all carry a version of ourselves we *want* others to see, confident, disciplined, reliable. You might believe you're someone who's always on time, but if you're constantly running late, the reality doesn't match the narrative. Self-awareness is about confronting those gaps. It's not about self-criticism; it's about seeing yourself clearly so you can create strategies that have a high probability of success.

Know What You're Good At (And What You're Not)

Self-awareness begins with a keen understanding of your gifts. We all have something we do exceptionally well. Some of us are born communicators, others thrive in building systems, solving problems, innovating, selling, negotiating, or leading.

But trying to win in areas you weren't built for is forcing a square peg into a round hole. Don't pull up to a traffic light in your Honda Accord and then challenge the Ferrari in the next lane to a race. Build a gameplan around your strengths. Then surround yourself with people and resources that offset your weaknesses and amplify your strengths. The key to tactical success and dominance is to set yourself up for victory BEFORE the battle is even fought. That's what self awareness allows you to do.

EQ > IQ

Emotional intelligence (EQ) is where the game elevates. It's knowing how you react under stress, how well you understand your emotions, and how attuned you are to others.

EQ is the reason some rise quickly and others stall. It shows up in negotiations, leadership moments, conflict resolution, and hiring decisions.

Ask yourself: What are my emotional triggers? What behavior patterns do I fall into during conflict? How do I respond when things don't go my way? The better you understand your own wiring, the more intentionally you can choose a course of action. This self-mastery is what separates the leaders from the followers, clearing the way for massive success.

The Four Levels of Self-Awareness

When I started my first career, selling investments and insurance products, I learned that people fall into four categories when it comes to self-awareness:

1. **The Conscious Competent**: You know you're an A-Player and you execute with precision. This is the person who knows their elite and operates accordingly.
2. **The Conscious Incompetent**: You know you have limitations and you don't try to fake it. You delegate, avoid overreaching and you play to your strengths with the humility to stay in your lane.
3. **The Unconscious Competent**: This is the guy with endless talent but he hasn't fully embraced his gifts. He doesn't even realize how good he is, settling for far less than he's capable of.
4. **The Unconscious Incompetent**: The most dangerous of all. They think they're good. They have no idea where their weaknesses lie. They get in over their heads, ignore feedback, and live in denial. They lose often.

Self-Awareness is the Path to Authenticity

In business, people gravitate toward those who are real. Not perfect. Not polished. Real. They want to work with people who know their strengths and weaknesses, play it well, and operate with humility. That's how you close deals, build teams, and lead movements. Self-awareness is what allows authenticity to show up without effort.

Most of us were taught to push feelings aside, especially when making decisions. Logic was king, and emotions were dismissed as distractions. But the truth is, when we ignore our feelings, we often end up chasing someone else's version of success instead of our own.

Your emotions are not the enemy of reason, they're your inner compass. They are your values. When something feels "off," that feeling is worth exploring. It's your intuition; the wisdom of experience and self-knowledge…nudging you toward alignment.

Start by including your emotions in the decision-making process. When faced with a choice, ask yourself, "How do I feel about this?" and just as importantly, "Why?" If a gut feeling is pushing back against what your rational mind is telling you, dig deeper. That friction is usually where the truth lives.

Make a habit of pausing, checking in, and allowing your emotions to have a seat at the table. Over time, this practice will sharpen your emotional intelligence and help you make decisions that are not only smart, but right for you.

One of the most transformative places to start is with your **energy**. Track your energy levels throughout the day for a few weeks. Note the times you feel focused, energized, and creative and when you feel depleted, distracted, or sluggish.

This simple practice will reveal your **peak performance windows**, those golden hours when you're naturally more productive and effective. These insights can revolutionize how you structure your day, helping you align your most important work with your highest energy, clearing the way for a major boost in productivity.

You'll also start to recognize the people, environments, and habits that fuel your energy…and the ones that drain it. With this knowledge, you can start creating a world that works *with* your biology, not against it.

Self-awareness isn't a destination, it's a practice. The more intentional you are about observing your passions, strengths and weaknesses, the more power you'll have.

Practicing self-awareness is not just a mental exercise, it's an act of self-leadership. It's how you bridge the gap between who you are now and who you're meant to become.

My Journey with Self-Awareness

I'm not perfect, but I know who I am. I know where I shine and where I struggle. I'm clear on what I bring to the table and what I need help with. That clarity is my competitive advantage. It helps me lead with confidence and speak with purpose. Self awareness is chess, not checkers.

Being self-aware has saved me from bad hires, bad deals, bad partnerships, and burnout. It's the compass I use in every major decision. When you're self-aware, you stop chasing validation and start chasing alignment. And when you're aligned, everything changes.

When we see ourselves clearly, we are more confident and more creative. We make sounder decisions, build stronger relationships, and communicate more effectively. We're less likely to lie, cheat, and steal. We are more-effective leaders with more-satisfied employees, more productive negotiations, and more-profitable companies.

Self-Awareness pays off in so many ways. If you're not good at math, don't major in accounting. If your hand-eye coordination is limited, don't plan for a career in baseball. If you're not attractive, skip the modelling career (sorry, somebody had to say it). Set yourself up to succeed. Play to your strengths. If you're not qualified for something, be humble enough to stay out of your own way.

A Few Ways to Improve Your Self-Awareness in Business

- Your reactions: Be aware of the way you respond physically, your listening face.
- Your attitudes: Know the vibe you put out during meetings.
- Your motives: Do you genuinely seek a win-win outcome?
- Your weaknesses: Acknowledge the things you lack or need to improve.

Your Call to Action

So here's your challenge: Know yourself better than anyone else. Audit your strengths. Be brutally honest about your blind spots. Ask for feedback. Reflect often. And most importantly, stay humble.

Set your ego aside, create game plans with a keen understanding of your strengths and weaknesses. Yes, we all have both.

Because in a world that's obsessed with noise, speed, and hype, self-awareness is your anchor. Your truth. It keeps you grounded, focused, and real. It attracts opportunity, elevates authenticity and bolsters your reputation. Self Awareness is your secret weapon on your road to the top, because you can't grow what you don't fully understand.

DON'T JUST BE AN IDEA GUY. EXECUTE!!

"

*"You can't build a reputation on
what you're going to do."*

Henry Ford

DON'T JUST BE AN "IDEA GUY". EXECUTE!!!

You're probably wondering what an "Idea Guy" is.

Now let's be clear for a minute. Ideas are important, especially the good ones. A good idea is the embryo of progress. Ideas build companies and solve problems.

So it might surprise you to hear that the *"Idea Guy"* label is something you need to avoid.

Here's the deal: The Idea Guy is full of suggestions, but the thing is, that same person rarely participates in the execution of the idea.

Idea Guys like to have meetings about what they recommend and how things can be done better. But that's usually where it ends. Idea Guys don't follow through, they rarely deliver, and they seldom provide anything… beyond the idea.

Be the guy who gets shit done. Merge your capacity to dream with a willingness to roll up your sleeves and work!!!

Be a Builder, Not Just a Brainstormer

Let's be honest, there's an addictive energy to brainstorming. Whiteboards, coffee shops, masterminds…it feels productive. People love to register new domain names, but so few of them become a fully developed website. Idea Guys love to name things and create logos.

But meaningful growth happens in the building process, the late nights, the trial and error. Real creation requires real risk and real time. That's where the idea becomes something real. A company. A brand. An invention. A movement. A legacy.

Don't romanticize the start. Fall in love with the **grind.**

I've known plenty of innovators who have come up with some really great ideas. My friend Lee Labrada came up with the idea of creating a great tasting, easily digestible line of meal replacement shakes. He called it *Lean Body*. Another friend, Aaron Singerman, had the idea of creating a high quality line of sports supplements built around patriotism; he named his company *RedCon1*. And let's not forget my friend Ryan DeLuca who came up with the idea of merging media and commerce to create a one-stop destination for nutritional products, long before Amazon entered the space. He called it Bodybuilding.com.

I could go on for days about men and women who have gone all-in, from idea to execution. I'm surrounded by some real-life success stories.

Those guys I mentioned are NOT idea guys. They are so much more! You see, they had the courage and the resolve to execute, turning their ideas into major companies, creating generational wealth.

Avoiding the "All Talk" label?

First, understand that it's a mindset. It's all about owning the moment. You can't wait for someone to hand you the map to the treasure—be the person who sets things in motion. Be the spark that brings ideas to life. The most successful people in my life got there because they took action, and along the way, they earned a reputation for their ability to get shit done.

There's a difference between passive hope and active drive. Michael Jordan famously said, "Some people want it to happen, some wish it would happen, others make it happen." It's really that simple.

Over time, ideas and promises become *noise*. Words can inspire, but execution earns respect—the kind of respect that others gravitate toward, bringing influence and opportunity into your life.

Know the Difference Between Input and Output

There's a trap in consuming too much without creating. I call them "Personal Development Junkies", the information hoarders. It's a common affliction. We all know those people. A casual addiction to podcasts, books, courses, seminars. They're all great. But at some point, all that input must convert to **output.**

If you read ten books, including this one, but launch nothing, you're just hoarding knowledge. Create more than you consume!!! Build more than you brainstorm. Work on it more than you talk about it.

Everyone Has Ideas

Let's not ignore the obvious. Everyone has ideas.

Everyone has a plan for a business, an app, a product, a movement. But what separates winners from wishers is the willingness to **take an idea off the whiteboard and bring it to life.**

Ideas don't pay the bills. They seldom generate revenue. They rarely attract investors. Execution is what gives your idea form, momentum, and value. It's not what's in your head, it's what you're willing to build.

In the startup phase, don't expect to get funding just for an idea. Investors or potential partners want to see something that's been brought to life, some early stage development -- even if it's just the initial pulse. A Venture Capital friend of mine *once told me "The value of most ideas is outweighed by the inconvenience of signing an NDA. So bring me more than an idea!!"*

It's not just the idea, it's the execution. Many successful companies got that way by strategically executing or repurposing an unoriginal idea. Starbucks didn't invent the notion of "fair trade coffee," any more than they were the first company to sell a cup of coffee. The iPod wasn't the first portable music player and Google wasn't the first monetizing search engine.

Most "Idea Guys" are just lazy, but not all of them. Here's a few of the factors that can take someone down the path of all talk, no action:

1. **Fear of Failure:** They get stuck in the theoretical, because "going for it" is risky.
2. **Perfection Paralysis:** They want the plan to be flawless before they begin.
3. **Validation Addiction:** They love the applause of sharing ideas more than the grind of making them happen.
4. **Lack of Follow-Through:** Discipline and consistency aren't nearly as easy as brainstorming.
5. **Over-Talking:** They spend all their time and energy talking about it, instead of shutting the fuck up and just doing the work.

Here's a quick reputation test: If you find yourself talking more about what you're "going to do" as opposed to what you've done, you might be slipping into *Idea Guy* territory. Be careful, it's a label that's hard to shed. People respect builders. They follow finishers. They invest in doers.

The Momentum Equation

Momentum is far more powerful than enthusiasm. Waiting for perfect conditions or perfect timing kills more dreams than failure ever will. Execution builds energy. It builds belief. And it creates momentum.

The key is simple: **start small and move fast.**

- Sketch the first version.

- Make the first call.
- Post the first announcement.
- Embrace feedback.
- Start building.

Done is better than perfect.

You won't figure it all out in advance. You figure it out as you go. You pivot, adjust, test, tweak…but you keep moving. And that's what separates you from the talkers.

Execution 101: The Basics

1. **Put It on the Calendar:** If it doesn't live on your schedule, it's not real.
2. **Hold Yourself Accountable:** Create deadlines, even when no one is watching.
3. **Replace the To-Do List With a "Must-Do" List:** Focus on a critical outcome for each day.
4. **Eliminate the Extras:** Cut meetings, cut fluff, cut anything not mission-critical.
5. **Track Action, Not Just Ideas:** Keep a journal of what actually got done.

No One Cares How Busy You Are!!!

I once had a VP job at a major publishing company, a fast paced, rapid fire environment, the kind of place where performance and productivity are closely measured. Each week, on Tuesdays, we would have a meeting comprised of all the various department heads. The purpose of the meeting was to update the CEO on various revenue generating initiatives. We would go around the room, one by one, to share key developments impacting cash flow, etc.. I still recall the first time I participated in the meeting. When it was my turn to talk, I spent about 10 uninterrupted minutes sharing details on the various deals and initiatives I was overseeing. When I finally finished talking, the CEO looked at me and said "Don't ever fucking do that again." As I tried to shield myself from the embarrassment of the moment, he added, "Next time, don't waste our time with details of what you're working on. None of those details are important. Just tell me what you've completed, what you've actually done. Nobody cares how busy you are!!!".

That experience changed me forever. We all walk around feeling like we're the busiest person in the room. Most people love talking about how busy they are, but busy doesn't mean shit and there's no trophies or pay checks for being busy. Successful people don't brag about being busy. It's all about true productivity, substance and real growth. Busy is just noise.

Listen More!!

Business leaders like Paul Allen, the founder of Ancestry.com, Howard Schultz, the founder of Starbucks, and Clifford Hudson, the CEO of Sonic Drive-Ins are execution guys. These guys know ideas are a dime a dozen and they keep their eyes and ears open.

Allen bought Ancestry and added publicly-available ancestry data, creating Ancestry.com. The company later sold for nearly 5 billion dollars. Schultz observed Italian cafes and brought the idea to the USA. Starbucks is currently valued at well over $100 billion. Hudson agreed to listen to a store owner about his self-made drink program. The program would double Sonic's size from one to two billion dollars from 1997-2001.

The victor is the better listener or the better observer, who simply executes on what others can't or won't scale. Steve Jobs famously said, "Good artists borrow, great artists steal" which is in itself a stolen quote from Pablo Picasso who said, "lesser artists borrow; great artists steal." To put it simply, it's not always about the idea. It's about the execution and the executor.

Build Your Reputation on Follow-Through

When it comes to reputation building, "follow-through" is a game changer, and sadly, it's one of the rarest attributes. The scary part about follow-through is that most people are in denial about it. People who don't follow-through seldom take ownership of it. If you end a meeting with the words, "Let's reconnect on Wednesday", then DO IT. Don't say it if you don't mean it.

Your word should be worth its weight in gold…and it starts with the smallest promises.

Execution isn't just about output. It's about **trust**. And trust opens doors that ideas never will.

Inspiration Without Discipline is Entertainment

Everyone loves the highlight reel. But most people don't love the systems, the spreadsheets, the calls, the notes, the rejection, the tracking.

That's where the real WINFUEL is found. The real players don't just dream big. **They execute small.** They break the goal into steps, and they do the work.

Don't be the guy everyone avoids because they know you'll pitch another idea that goes nowhere. Be the one they call because they know you'll get it done.

Talk less. Do more. Follow through. That's how you build a reputation, the kind that attracts more opportunities. That's how you win, over and over again.

BUILD A THINK TANK

"Smart people learn from everything and everyone, average people learn from their experiences, and stupid people already have all the answers."

Socrates

BUILD A THINK TANK

The most successful people in the world have them.

They're powerful. Dependable. Incredibly valuable. They can help you navigate to new heights, while also taking the most challenging situations in for a smooth landing. No, we're NOT talking about a private jet.

We're talking about something far more impactful, **a Think Tank**.

It's the business-world equivalent of an inner-circle. A personal advisory board. A curated council of minds that help you move faster, smarter, and with far more confidence than you ever could alone.

At its core, a Think Tank is about elevated decision-making through trusted collaboration. Building a good one isn't easy, but those who have one are infinitely more likely to soar higher.

An Underrated Asset

Most people believe success comes from hustle, skill, timing, and sometimes, luck. Of course all of those things are a part of the equation. But what separates those who plateau from those who reach another level of influence and impact is one thing -- they never stop learning, and they surround themselves with smarter, wiser people.

It's not about surrounding yourself with "yes" people. It's about surrounding yourself with *wisdom and intuition*, those who challenge you, inspire you, and care deeply about your success.

A true Think Tank acts as:

- A **sounding board** for your biggest ideas and toughest decisions.
- A **mirror** to reflect blind spots, biases, or the traps created by ego.
- A **filter** to help you evaluate opportunity and risk.
- A **strategic council** that helps you think beyond your default patterns.

The Essential Qualities of a Think Tank Member

A Think Tank isn't just a group of accomplished people. It's a very *intentional* selection of individuals with a blend of the following attributes:

1. Wisdom & Experience
They've been in the trenches. They've made the hard calls. They've built, lost, rebuilt, and learned. Their advice comes from *doing*, not just theory.

2. Clarity & Instincts
They see patterns others miss. They can break down a complex problem and offer fresh perspective. They're clear thinkers and excellent communicators.

3. Courage & Honesty

They're not afraid to tell you when you're wrong, or when your idea needs refining. They value *truth* over flattery.

4. Humility

They don't pretend to know it all. They're open to learning from *you*, too. A good Think Tank is a *mutual elevation machine*.

5. Loyalty & Discretion

They protect your vision, your vulnerabilities, and your reputation. What's said in the tank, stays in the tank.

6. Alignment of Values

They may come from different backgrounds or industries, but they share your *values* and your hunger.

Not every "smart & successful friend" qualifies. Choose carefully. Trust is the central artery of every Think Tank.

Make Sure They Genuinely Want You to Win!!!

This is where things get tricky. We all know some incredibly smart, dynamic and accomplished individuals. Personally, I've built a network loaded with power players who have built massive companies and generational wealth, men and women who have achieved at the highest level. But not everyone is built to be in a Think Tank. The truth is, not everyone wants you to win….and not everyone wants me to win. It's the nature of the beast. Many of the world's most successful people are not wired to be concerned about anyone's success but their own. This doesn't make them bad people, it's simply a byproduct of the unique circumstances of their life, or how they were raised, or how secure they are in what they've built.

That's what makes a good Think Tank difficult to build. Identifying smart and successful friends is the easy part. But finding individuals who genuinely want you to win is a bit more challenging. The world is competitive. Even your closest friends can be territorial. Not everyone is generous with their wisdom.

Let your instincts guide you. Ask yourself some hard questions:

- Do they push you to be better, do they challenge you?
- How do they speak of you when you're not around?
- Do they prefer to compete or collaborate?
- Are they willing to tell you what you might not want to hear?
- Do they celebrate your wins in a way that feels sincere?
- Do they have your back, even when it's inconvenient?
- Are they secure enough to truly contribute to your Think Tank?

Remember, a friend can still be a friend, even if they aren't a good fit for your Think Tank. Not all relationships are the same. Proceed accordingly.

My Think Tank

In my world, there are several verticals that require occasional reinforcement. As a company president, I'll seek input from someone who understands the unique challenges of balancing audience development with revenue objectives, overall production and fan experience. As an investor, I keep an open line of communication with someone who has a keen understanding of the global markets, asset allocation and risk management. And as a marketer, I've built some highly collaborative relationships with some influential, smart and dynamic individuals who know how to connect with people in a powerful way.

As much as I enjoy learning from them, the most fulfilling moments come when I'm able to contribute to the success of those in my Think Tank. Giving is far more gratifying than receiving. I've watched members of my inner-circle close massive deals because of tactical input I've provided or because I was able to bring the right people together. My Think Tank is a treasure trove of wisdom, loyalty and most importantly, insanely good energy!! And if you're wondering why I'm not mentioning their names, it's because discretion is a big part of what makes my Think Tank work. Yours might be different. No two are the same.

If You Don't Already Have One...

There's no "How To" manual for building a think tank. It's generally an organic process, one born from years of relationship building and life experience, combined with an instinctive sense of trust.

You don't want clones. You want selected individuals who offer what you don't. If you're great at product development but weak on financial strategy, a CFO-type might be a nice fit. If you're a strong visionary but lack operational instincts, bring in someone organizational-minded, a company builder!!

Don't be over-eager to build your Think Tank. It takes time. Identify those who operate with **respectful candor** and *minimal ego*. This isn't about showmanship, it's about elevation.

The Pillars of a Good Think Tank

1. Transparency
If you're not honest about what's really going on, no one can help you. Be open. Be real. It's a safe zone.

2. Reciprocity
You're not just a taker. Deliver value back. Offer insight. Share wins. Make introductions. *Serve* the people who serve you.

3. Follow-Through
If your group gives you insight or feedback, act on it and let them know how it played out.

4. Gratitude
Thank your Think Tank often. A note, a gift, a shoutout, small acts of appreciation keep the circle strong.

The Benefits

Practical ways a Think Tank will elevate your game.

1. Enhance Decision-Making

Make sharper, faster, more strategic decisions when you bounce ideas off others with proven abilities to make good things great, or big problems small.

2. Fuel Creativity

Diverse minds bring diverse ideas. Your Think Tank will help you break out of ruts and think more innovatively.

3. Expand Your Network

A good Think Tank is supercharged by the combined value of everyone's individual network, allowing opportunities to multiply, giving way to unexpected partnerships, investors, talent, or promotional opportunities.

4. Provide Emotional Resilience

It's lonely at the top. Your Think Tank gives you a place to exhale. To vent. To be supported without judgment.

5. Hold You Accountable

They'll challenge your excuses and celebrate your progress. The kind of accountability that drives momentum and raises your game.

Examples of Think Tanks in Action

- **Warren Buffett and Charlie Munger** – The ultimate two-man Think Tank. Their long standing partnership has shaped the investment world, driven by brutal honesty, curiosity, and mutual trust.
- **Oprah Winfrey's Brain Trust** – Oprah credits her billion dollar empire to a core circle of mentors, producers, and spiritual advisors who've helped guide her business for decades.
- **Silicon Valley Founders** – Most major tech entrepreneurs operate within informal Think Tanks, text groups, dinners, and meetups where strategy, talent, and ideas are exchanged.
- **Mastermind Groups** – From Napoleon Hill's *Think and Grow Rich* to today's billionaire retreats, the concept of gathering high-level thinkers for mutual growth is a timeless formula.

Warning: Avoid These Types!!!

This isn't about popularity or even proximity. Your Think Tank should feel like a strategic sanctuary, a place of depth, trust, and even a little inspiration.

A few types of individuals to *avoid*:

- **The Naysayer**: Always negative, rarely constructive. Drains momentum.
- **The "Yes" Person**: Never challenges you. Always agrees. Adds little value.

- **The Ego-Driven**: Competes with you instead of collaborating. Toxic.
- **The Overcommitted**: They love you, but never follow through. Inconsistent.

Your Legacy

The longer you nurture your Think Tank, the more powerful it becomes. Over time, it becomes more than just a support group, it becomes a *legacy network* --helping you shape not just what you do, but who you become and how the world sees you.

- They help you *see yourself* clearly when the world is noisy.
- They remind you *who you are* when you lose your way.
- They elevate your *thinking*, which elevates your life.

Start Building Yours

Don't rush the process. As I mentioned earlier, the creation of your Think Tank shouldn't be forced. It's a natural alignment of the right energy and the right intentions. But if you're in a rush, here's a few ways to go about it:

- Identify 3–5 trusted, high-caliber people in your network who could help you grow. Individuals who genuinely want you to win.
- Reach out and schedule a call or coffee to explore it further.
- Create a group text or forum where ideas and support can flow.

- Bring a real problem or scenario to the table, take your tank for a test drive.
- Invest in their success as much as they do in yours.

This isn't just about building a network. It's about adding horsepower. Winfuel.

A carefully crafted Think Tank is the ultimate Winfuel. It multiplies your ideas, accelerates growth, and protects your weak spots. So build your Think Tank. Nurture it. Protect it.

And when it's done right, you'll realize it's not just a secret weapon. It's a protective layer, a competitive edge, and most importantly, it's the most cost-effective talent acquisition you'll ever make.

SEE IT THROUGH
THEIR EYES

"Seek first to understand, then to be understood"

Stephen Covey

SEE IT THROUGH THEIR EYES

Everyone dreams of having a superpower. If given the choice, what would yours be?

Some would choose the ability to fly. Others might choose the power to be invisible. I have friends at the gym who would go with "superhero strength" as their superpower. The list goes on. So many intriguing options.

But for me, I'd choose something far more useful, and infinitely more valuable.

The power to see the world through the eyes of other people.

What makes this superpower so unique is that it's not a fantasy, it's actually within our reach, if we allow ourselves to do it. It's not an easy skill to develop. It takes time. But even more than that, it demands a specific mindset, one rooted in curiosity, humility, and a sincere desire to *understand….before being understood*.

The truth? Most people spend their lives obsessed with being heard, validated, or admired. But those who reach the top, they don't just communicate well. They *connect deeply*. They don't just listen. They *tune in*.

Empathy: Your Competitive Advantage

Empathy isn't weakness. It isn't soft. It's not about becoming a pushover.

Empathy is *data*. It's *intelligence*. It's *strategy*.

When you can understand what another person values, fears, hopes for, and needs, you can tailor your approach to build trust, resolve conflict, and create powerful outcomes. It's how deals get done and partnerships are developed.

Think about it:

- The salesperson who understands the *real* hesitation behind the buyer's objection will close more deals than the one who just sells harder.
- The leader who senses when an employee is burning out will attract and retain top talent.
- The negotiator who sees through ego and hears what's *not* being said will craft win-win solutions, while others get stuck in a power struggle.

A Highly Underrated Secret Weapon!

The first step toward building a culture of opportunity and influence is to harness the tactical advantages of empathy. Understanding and appreciating the challenges, aspirations and perspectives of others can transform competitive interaction into collaborative opportunity.

A good leader can initiate this by actively listening to their teams, partners and even competitors, seeking to understand **before** being understood. This approach not only enhances morale but also opens avenues for problem-solving and growth.

Perspective is Wisdom

When you look only through your own lens, everything is colored by your goals, your values, and your pain points. That's natural, we all have our filters.

But the moment you pause and ask, *"What does this look like from their side?"* everything changes.

Let's say you're in a tough negotiation. You're focused on margin, deliverables, and timelines. But the person across the table is worried about reputation, internal politics, or simply not losing face in front of their followers. If you miss that perspective, you'll press the wrong buttons.

Try stepping into their shoes. What keeps them up at night? Who are they accountable to? What's their version of a "win"? What emotional driver lives beneath their words?

When you start asking these questions, you stop guessing and start *connecting*.

And in a world that's becoming more automated and transactional by the day, real *connection has never been more scarce. And more valuable.*

Muscle Business, My World

In the competitive world of fitness commerce, companies are constantly in search of opportunities to reach high volume audiences. The market is flooded with brands maneuvering to differentiate themselves from their competitors. Each of them seeking to increase visibility, engagement and most importantly – sales!! As president of the most influential event brand in the category I work closely with CEO's and marketing directors, each looking to capitalize on the dedicated fit minded men and women who follow and attend the Olympia. But in order for me to help them grow, it's critical that I allow myself to fully understand their unique objectives. No two companies are the same. Each has their own story, their own track record of success and failure. Each company has a different definition of a winning transaction. For some, it's simply a matter of branding, ensuring that their company is known by as many people as possible. For others, the objectives are more specific:

- Connect with as many 18-25 year old bodybuilders as possible.
- Get physical products in as many hands as possible.
- Collect data; email addresses, phone numbers, etc..
- Grow their social media following and improve engagement.
- Convert their sponsorship spend to actual on-site sales.
- Educate the community about a new product or ingredient.
- Shine a spotlight on their company's ownership or vision.
- Collect enough video to fuel their content pipeline.

The list goes on.

In order to identify the best course of action, it's vital that I understand the objectives. In certain cases, it calls for a basic event activation. For others, my team will deploy media resources and other targeted programs aimed at achieving a desired outcome. There's nothing "boiler plate" about it. Everyone is different.

Over the years I've been fortunate to develop countless long-standing client relationships. Companies and executives who come back year after year to execute the kind of growth strategies that give way to measurable shifts in momentum. I'm not trying to sell them anything. I work to solve something for them. They keep coming back because I spend valuable time listening, understanding, collaborating – seeing it through their eyes.

Listen for What's Not Being Said

Listening. It's not just about nodding and not interrupting. It's about reading body language, noticing tone changes, and perhaps even more valuable, **observing the topics that are being avoided**. There is tremendous power in detecting unspoken fears and motivations.

Let's say you're in a sales situation and a potential client says, "This sounds great, but I'm not sure we're ready." You could take that at face value. Or you could lean in and say:

"I get that. When you say 'not ready,' do you mean operationally, financially, or emotionally? I want to make sure we're solving the right problem."

That one simple question does three things:

1. It shows you're paying attention.
2. It Invites vulnerability.
3. It gets the conversation closer to the finish line.

When people feel truly *seen*, they stop hiding. And when they stop hiding, you stop guessing. To further understand this, take note of the idea that there are different levels of listening:

Distracted Conventional Listening[1]

"Level One Listening" is ordinary, general listening. Some might call it superficial. While the other person is speaking we may zone out briefly, easily distracted by other thoughts and ideas. Instead of fully engaging, we wait for our turn to speak, thinking about what we'll say next. We're listening as much, or more, to our inner voice as we are the person who is speaking.

Focused Active Listening

"Level Two Listening" is what most people are doing when they say they are good "active listeners". We are focused on the speaker and concentrating on what that person has to say. We are engaged with the person speaking — nodding and maintaining eye contact. We shut down our inner voice, and try not to run a parallel conversation internally about responses, judgment, or when it will be our turn to speak.

---

[1] https://ardencoaching.com/beyond-active-listening-the-power-of-level-three-listening/

Profoundly Connected Listening

"Level three Listening" connects you more deeply and more holistically to the person you're talking to. A level three listener takes everything into account in the moment — what the speaker is saying, their body language, their tone of voice, the environment, the circumstances of the conversation, and what they're feeling and observing in response.

Level three listening takes into account how, why, when and where they are saying it. It requires practice, keen intuition, and a soft focus. This level of listening is easier said than done, but if you can get there it's a massive game changer.

Emotional Context

All decisions, especially in high-stakes business, are emotional before they're logical. People justify with data, but they decide with emotion.

They agree to your terms because they trust you. They partner because they feel respected. They walk away because something *felt* off, even if the numbers were perfect. To see through someone's eyes is to understand their *emotional context*. Is this deal about protecting their job? Proving something to a boss? Finally feeling heard after being overlooked? Achieving some kind of social validation?

Empathy isn't about manipulation. It's about recognizing what's *real*, so you can strategize, influence, and solve problems.

When you see someone's world clearly, you become the person they *trust* to help them change it.

When Their "Eyes" Are Nothing Like Yours

Let's address a more complex scenario: Sometimes it's hard to see through someone else's eyes because their worldview is *completely different* than yours. Different background. Different values. Different communication style. This is where true mastery begins.

Empathy isn't agreement. It's *understanding*.

Despite popular belief, you can grasp someone's perspective without compromising your own values. In fact, understanding *why* they see things differently will often help you find common ground that logic never could. This is true with religion, politics and BUSINESS.

Let's say you're managing a multigenerational team. Your Gen Z employee values flexibility, purpose, and mental health. Your Gen X executive values structure, loyalty, and measurable output.

Both are right. Both are valid. But if you only see through one lens, the other will feel unseen.

As a leader or a boss you must allow yourself to ask:

- *"What does the world look like from where they stand?"*
- *"What are they protecting, preserving, or hoping to prove?"*
- *"What pain or pride are they bringing into this conversation?"*

When you can sit with someone who is radically different from you and *understand them anyway*, you've unlocked one of the rarest skills in the world, and one of the most valuable.

Let's Talk About Conflict

Most people approach conflict like a courtroom. They want to win. They build their case. They wait to debate, not to understand. But if you want to de-escalate a situation and move forward, don't just explain your side. Reflect theirs, allow them to feel seen.

Empathy in conflict management goes beyond mere understanding. It involves actively engaging with another person's perspective. This kind of engagement can transform conflict dynamics by breaking down barriers of defensiveness and misunderstanding.

When parties in a conflict feel understood, they are more likely to open up to finding the kind of common ground that leads to a valuable outcome. When empathy is present, individuals are more likely to think creatively and collaboratively. Understanding the needs and concerns of all parties allows for the development of solutions, a true source of Winfuel.

Practice: The "Mirror and Window" Method

In every professional encounter, make a real effort to assess what you are putting out as well as what you're receiving.

- **The Mirror**: *What's my body language, tone, wardrobe, intensity and energy* projecting onto this person? Be honest with yourself. What are they seeing, what are they hearing when you're talking?
- **The Window**: What am I learning about their world, their objectives and their priorities?

This helps you separate assumptions from reality. Go two layers deep. When someone shares an objection, don't stop at the first layer.

- "What makes that important to you?"
- "Tell me more about why that's a concern."

Go deeper. That's where the gold is. Over time, this level of awareness and exploration becomes instinctive.

When You Master This, You'll Win Bigger & More Often

Here's what happens when you learn to truly see through their eyes:

- You stop selling and start solving.
- You stop chasing people and start attracting them.
- You stop defending your ideas and start *designing better ones*, with others.
- You build trust faster.
- You lead from clarity, not ego.
- You create outcomes that last, because everyone feels invested.

Real Power, Real People

At the end of the day, this isn't about becoming a saint. You won't always get it right. There will be times when ego sneaks in, when you're too rushed to be fully present. But the more you return to the practice, the more you train yourself to pause and truly listen, the more you'll become someone who doesn't just *win*...

You'll become someone people *want to win with*.

This is where *winning* starts to multiply. Wins turn into more wins, transactions evolve into sustainable partnerships – a powerful pathway to the kind of reputation that can elevate you to the top of your industry.

So the next time you're in a conversation, meeting, negotiation, or even a disagreement, don't just think about your angle. Ask yourself:

"What does this look like from where they're standing?"

Because true VISION goes far beyond what you see. It's the ability to see the world through a set of eyes that don't even belong to you. That's not just power. That's a superpower.

CONSISTENCY
IS KING

"People don't follow the occasional spark.
They follow the steady flame."

Robin Sharma

CONSISTENCY IS KING

For many of you, buying this book occurred during a surge in personal growth. You're eager, you're hungry, and you're ready to up your game. You're working harder than you've worked before, more focused, more energized. And while this is commendable, for many of you, this window will soon close. You'll become distracted, focus will shift, energy will change, and you'll revert back to the way you were. I don't mean to be a buzz kill, but most people are hot and cold. One month you're all in, the next month you're back to your old habits. It's the reason many of your brightest friends **never** reached their potential. They had all the tools they needed, but they never built a sustainable process. Their dreams were bigger than their discipline and their focus.

Listen closely. Success isn't a destination. It's the creation of habits, a series of small, measurable actions that grow like compounding interest. It isn't flashy, it's repetitive and habit-forming. While you can't control every outcome, you have full control over the choices you make each day. Temporary intensity might clear the way for a homerun, but it won't turn you into a *"homerun hitter"*. My baseball friends will understand the difference.

The Reputation Builder

Consistency isn't just about growth and performance, it's about building a personal brand – a reputation!! Reliability builds trust –

for your company, your product, and for how the world perceives you. **Consistency is a form of trust**, a demonstration of commitment and dependability. People gravitate to those with a pattern of sustainable performance. Major deals are closed when patterns of consistent performance, behavior, and productivity are identified by those around you.

The Power of Patterns

In every high-stakes opportunity, people are quietly watching your *patterns.* Not your moments. People want to do business with patterns they can trust, not fireworks they can't predict. If you want more responsibility, more investment, more influence…
Start by building *better patterns.*

The truth is, most people aren't consistent. They live in cycles of high ambition…then burnout. Big talk…then excuses. A never-ending cycle.

This is why consistent performers are *rare.* And in business, *rarity is value.* Reliability is in high demand, across every industry. And because so few can sustain long-term effort, *your ability to stay consistent makes you unstoppable, and coveted.*

Be the one who *shows up,* every day, every week, every season.

It's the thing no one talks about. Consistency isn't just about habits. It's a mindset built on a clear reason *why* you're doing what you're doing and a set of standards that override your moods.

Sets & Reps

One of the perks of decades spent in the business of fitness is the constant reminder that consistency is transformational. The gym teaches us this. Championship physiques aren't built from the occasionally spectacular workout. They come from a day in and day out commitment. One rep, one set, one workout at a time. It's the daily infusion of blood into the muscle that delivers nutrients and oxygen, stretching the fascia, signaling the body to initiate a repair and growth process. Over time, the consistent delivery of blood creates the anabolic environment that causes the muscle to grow and the body to change.

Just like in business, the real work happens when few are watching. The pain and the burn of each rep creates small changes. Over time, the small changes add up to noticeable improvements. But it all starts with consistency. It's physiology's version of compounding interest.

Some of the most successful people I know started their journey in the gym. It's where they first came to understand the power of dedication and the concept of how small things add up to big things. Many of them applied these lessons to build companies that reached multi-nine-figure valuations. Consistency is the embryo of influence and wealth. It starts with a mindset, an attitude, and a willingness to show up.

It's Not a Destination

Stop viewing success as a place you're trying to get to....and **start viewing it as the repetition of high-value behaviors that**

compound over time. It isn't flashy. It's not overnight and it's not built on viral moments. It's built on the routine, repetitive stuff that most under-value:

- Showing up when no one's watching
- Executing even when you don't feel like it
- Performing on low energy days
- Doing the basics better than anyone else

The flashiest performers get temporary attention. The most consistent ones build something greater. Reliability is a brand. A powerful one. It says, "You can trust me, I'm dependable" and it sends a message that you don't disappear when things get hard.

This isn't just about work ethic, it's about identity. When people know they can count on you, doors open. Deals get done. Partnerships are built. Status elevates. In business, consistency isn't just competence. It's productivity, credibility and sometimes – it's power.

What Consistency Really Looks Like

Let's be real: consistency isn't glamorous. It's steady communication. It's keeping promises, especially the ones you make to yourself. It's operating with discipline, not dopamine, the neurotransmitter that chases stimulation and thrives on temporary bursts of excitement.

You might have spurts of inspiration. You might have months where you're "on fire." But what creates real transformation? **Making it**

your Identity. That means consistency isn't something you *do*, it's something you *become.* It's a mindset.

Consistency to Build Influence

It's a simple idea. Prominence in business happens when you go from being someone they recognize to someone they rely on. That's where consistency comes in. In a world filled with noise and uncertainty, being consistent with your message, your performance and your habits is how you become trusted. Consistency separates those who get noticed from those who are remembered. It's not just showing up when you want to, it's showing up when you'd rather be somewhere else. Nearly everything in business is erratic, the economy, the markets, and the temperament of your clients and followers. The key is to position yourself as the steady hand in a world filled with volatility. Consistency amplifies everything you do. It builds belief and momentum. And over time, it builds something more powerful. Influence.

Let Me Spell It Out For You!!!

W – Write down your top non-negotiable behaviors

I – Identify triggers that cause inconsistency

N – Neutralize distractions in your environment

F – Focus on input, not outcome

U – Upgrade your routine as you grow

E – Execute even when it's boring

L – Lead by example

Be the Minority

The world is filled with people who show bursts of energy, temporary ambition, and short-lived productivity. They're a dime a dozen. They start strong, then they fade. We see it in all parts of life. It's the reason why every gym in America is crowded during the first few days of January. Big goals and resolutions give way to a temporary surge in effort, followed by diminished focus, and the inevitable return to the same mindset that held them back to begin with. The same is common in business. They show up when it's new and exciting, but they pull back when things get challenging or when it feels repetitive.

Here's the truth. Consistency is hard. It requires resilience and a deeply rooted purpose, the kind of purpose that over-powers distractions. It's a mental game and not everyone is built for it. This is why consistent people are so valuable. It's a matter of supply and demand. The demand for consistent performers is far greater than the supply. And reliability is more valuable than random brilliance. Consistency is your Winfuel, it's what I look for in those I do business with and those who I hire. In the end, consistent performance is hard to replace, but more importantly, it's the surest way to win.

The Great Separator

When it's not sexy, when it's not new, when it's not exciting, that's when *consistency* becomes your advantage. Because most people *slow down* when the initial shine wears off. But those who operate at a higher level lock-in. This is the great separator.

They double down on the behaviors that matter. They bet on their routines.

They show up when no one's around to cheer. And they do it again and again and again, until they're on top.

So if you're wondering what your next move is, it's simple:

Be the one who keeps showing up, the one who follows through, the one who consistently delivers. Consistency isn't easy. But it's powerful. It builds reputations and cultivates trust. It creates wealth. It builds brands. And it creates legacies.

THE POWER OF
THE PIVOT

"Those who can't change their minds,
can't change anything"

George Bernard Shaw

THE POWER OF THE PIVOT

If you're 50 years old, the words on these pages might look different than if you're 25. Not just blurrier…different.

Different because adapting to change is a topic that's met with varying degrees of interest. There are some who have an intense appetite for the latest trends in technology and efficiency, always embracing new ways to do things. And then there are those who want no part of it. They cling to the familiar like a raft, resisting change regardless of the potential benefit.

Full disclosure: This chapter is a cautionary letter to those of you who struggle with change. I'll try my best to keep it friendly, but sometimes tough love is what it takes.

No matter your age, there are few things more important than *adapting, shifting*, and sometimes recalibrating. The power of the pivot is real. It's much like when your iPhone tells you it's time to do an update. If you repeatedly ignore the update, eventually the performance of the device begins to break down.

As time passes, the algorithm of human behavior changes. The concept of value changes as well as the way we share information, solve problems, and connect with each other. Our priorities change too.

Artificial Intelligence has become *assisted* intelligence because there's truly nothing artificial about it. It's real. It's powerful. And it's redefining every industry. Those who see it, welcome it, and use it, will dominate. Those who dismiss it or fear it? They'll be at a massive disadvantage.

But pivoting goes far beyond technology. Sometimes it's as simple as having the humility to change your mind or re-strategize. The best football coaches know how to assess changes in the opposing defense. The game plan may have helped you win last week, but this week's game comes with different variables. The field conditions may have changed, the temperature isn't the same, and sometimes, in certain cases, the rules aren't even the same.

Last week's game plan got you an easy win, but winning today may require a new strategy and a new vision. Those who have the capacity to see it will keep winning.

Those who refuse to pivot will be left to look back on the "good old days." -- Don't be that guy.

A Balancing Act

When it comes to navigating a rapidly changing business world, the challenge is to leverage innovation without losing yourself in the process. It's a bit of a balancing act. Don't disconnect from the fundamentals that got you to this point. Stay true to those core values. Continue to be you, but don't fall behind.

The path to big wins lies in your ability to maintain your identity while supercharging your growth. This isn't about chasing trends and forgetting who you are. It's about being the business version of *bigger/faster/stronger*.

Change is only threatening when you don't know who you are. Root yourself in your core values…and let those values guide you through the pivot.

Adapting and evolving isn't just about technology. Sometimes it's about strategy, the need to pivot toward larger audiences and new customers. When the Mr. Olympia was created back in the 1960's, it was simply a bodybuilding competition. While it stood proudly as the most coveted title in the world of muscle, its focus was limited and its audience craved just one thing. Muscle.

As the years passed, health & fitness became incredibly popular in ways that went far beyond biceps and protein powder. Sports nutrition reached new levels of innovation. Women became a dominant force on the fitness scene and new trends were emerging in martial arts, endurance sports, Pilates, apparel, CrossFit, and exercise equipment. It all added up to massive demand and significant consumer spending. Olympia creator Joe Weider saw the shift and decided to re-brand his Mr. Olympia into something inclusive of all things fitness. Today, the event is called Joe Weider's Olympia Fitness & Performance Weekend, a multi-day experience held on more than a half a million square feet of convention center space, a gathering place for top brands, celebrities, content creators, and a long list of fitness themed events. It was the ultimate pivot.

Don't Overthink it!!

Unless you've been living under a rock, you're already aware of what's happening in the world of artificial intelligence. While those words are scary to some of you, I'm gonna let you in on a little secret:

The reason AI has become so widely utilized is because it was designed to be useful for everyone, even you!! With just a few taps, ANYONE can access an entire world of support, information and expertise— without a learning curve. Services like ChatGPT and a long list of "productivity apps" are allowing users to access the kind of efficiency, creativity and high-level thinking that once seemed unimaginable. **The ease of use has leveled the playing field**, giving start-ups and under-funded businesses the chance to grow without increasing payroll. Tasks that once required days and weeks are now being completed in minutes, at no cost. Companies are using user-friendly AI to create pitch decks, perform market research, create sales scripts and design promotional graphics. But that's just the beginning. AI is being used to convert marketing videos into hundreds of different languages with just a push of a button, while also creating written summaries of long meetings and brain storming new ideas.

I won't use these pages to share all the ways these tools can help you grow, but I'll simply let you know that you'll eventually get crushed if you don't embrace it. AI is no longer a luxury item. It's a fundamental part of modern business. If you're among the stubborn, this is where you need to wake-the-fuk-up!!!

Take it Slow if Needed

The key to all of this is progress. One step at a time. Gradually embrace new processes and new technology. Allow yourself and your team to adapt. A gradual ramp-up will help minimize resistance. Over time, the small steps will add up and with each passing month you'll achieve new levels of efficiency and productivity. And here's the best part. When you allow yourself to ride the wave, your brain will gradually begin doing things it hadn't done before, identifying new ways to grow, new opportunities. You'll become something different. You'll discover something within yourself that you never knew was there. But it all starts with a few gradual moves.

Stubborn is Not a Compliment!!!

Many of the things that once seemed optional are now essential. Being stubborn about learning new ways to grow is just a disguised version of fear. In the business world, refusal to embrace innovation is like choosing to run uphill, with bricks tied to your ankles!! Not only does it slow your progress, but it also sends a dangerous message to those who are watching you. To be candid, it makes you look foolish.

The dictionary defines stubborn as "Someone who's unwilling to change their mind, attitude or behavior".

No one wants to work with a dinosaur, let alone a stubborn one. Your team is watching. Your clients are watching. Your competitors are watching. A stubborn leader resists change, clinging to outdated methods, while the world moves forward.

Reputational Capital

There's another layer to this that needs to be considered. Your ability to evolve and pivot is an intangible asset, impacting how others perceive you.

Do your clients view you as someone who's open to new ways of thinking? Do your followers see you as someone who can deliver relevant, present-day value? Will potential partners or employees view you as someone who can guide them in a world of constant change?

The dominant brands of the future won't be the ones that mastered yesterday's platforms. They'll be the ones that continued to learn, continued to evolve, and stayed current, without selling out.

Those who welcome change stand out as leaders. The future belongs to those who are adaptable. You've gotten this far because you're dedicated, passionate and smart. But the game is constantly changing and yesterday's wins......are yesterday's wins.

The Courage to Reinvent

You will never know how far you can go until you let go of who you used to be. Some will try to guilt you into staying the same. They'll say, "You've changed." And you know what? You should!! You should change. You should evolve. You should reinvent. Not just once, but over and over again.

Every season of your professional evolution requires a different version of you. **The pivot is not a betrayal of who you were—it's a commitment to who you're becoming.**

If we're being honest, we can admit that change has its challenges. The *decision* to change isn't hard; it's the actual work that goes into changing that's hard. On top of that, it's the fear that we talked about earlier in the book.

Let's be real: Self-improvement requires change. Healing requires change. Physical fitness and emotional health require change. And being a good leader, that requires change too. So embracing change in business is crucial.

Adaptation as a Competitive Advantage

Look around at the companies, entrepreneurs, and creators who are winning right now. They're not just brilliant. They're *responsive.* They read the signs. They track the data. They study culture. And they adjust accordingly.

They test and they tweak. They're not married to their pride. They're married to the mission. Pivoting isn't weakness. It's wisdom. In the words of Dr. Wayne Dyer, someone I admired very much, "Have a mind that is opened to everything and attached to nothing". This doesn't mean that you should have no soul. It's a mindset. It encourages openness and the avoidance of limited thinking. Stay curious and be flexible.

You don't need to overhaul your business every quarter. You don't need to chase every new platform or trend. But you *do* need to stay awake. You *do* need to keep learning. And you *do* need to be willing to evolve.

Because change isn't coming. It's here…and the world is watching you.

TRAIN YOUR MIND TO BE STRONGER THAN YOUR FEELINGS

"

*"Control your emotions,
or they will control you."*

Napolean Hill

TRAIN YOUR MIND TO BE STRONGER THAN YOUR FEELINGS

The 12th Secret. This is a big one. It's a constant battle, the source of nearly all your indecision and internal conflict. A showdown between the two most dominant forces in your life. Your brain and your heart.

There's a lot of ground to cover here, but similar to our chapter on fear, it starts with **control**.

Control over your emotions, your thoughts, your body language, and your words. Calm emotion creates calm energy and calm energy exudes confidence. Let's get straight to the point. Controlling your emotions doesn't mean denying them.

It means *directing* them. It means *understanding* where they come from and *deciding* how to channel them. Logic vs Emotion. Analysis vs Instincts. Let's explore it together.

Your emotional state is like a transmitter. It sends signals, across the room, the stage, the Zoom call, or the dinner table.

People often feel your energy **before** they process your words.

That means that if you radiate confidence, others lean in. If you radiate panic, others pull back. If you're composed, you create clarity. If you're reactive, you create chaos.

Leaders who win, the ones who consistently outperform, excel in the art of staying calm when others can't. They stay grounded. And in doing so, they soar above the panic, the emotion and the nonsense.

Composure becomes your WINFUEL.

When Feelings Cause Damage

Training your mind to be stronger than your feelings is about putting your brain power to work, ensuring that your years of experience, education and wisdom aren't minimized by the tug of emotional sentiment. It's nearly impossible to be an effective leader if the nostalgia of a friendship leads you to over-value someone's ability to perform. Just as it's difficult to execute sound business transactions when your *feelings* cloud your ability to measure value– real, quantifiable value.

I've often said, if you're shopping for a new home, it would be foolish to choose a house because you really liked the realtor. That's the kind of thinking that gets you in trouble. Because after the deal closes and the realtor is long gone, you'll still be living in the house, the victim of allowing your feelings to lead the way.

But what about the people who told you to follow your heart?

This is where things get a bit more complicated. The heart can't be ignored. It's where passion lives. It's also where instincts begin. It would be ridiculous if I advised you to ignore the quiet sparks from deep within, the kind that can turn into flames, otherwise known as a burning desire. But the most successful people understand how to use those emotional signals to provide key information that the brain can use to help determine what truly matters to them. Some might say that your heart provides the "why" while your brain takes care of the "how".

Calm is Contagious

In the world of a NAVY SEAL, discipline, mental toughness and teamwork can be the difference between life and death. *"Calm is Contagious"*, it's a phrase you'll often hear among the SEALS. Critical advice about the need to stay cool when the stakes are at their highest, underscoring the danger of losing your cool during the most intensely challenging moments, making rash decisions with little thought and a lot of emotion.

Keeping people calm as a leader, an advisor, or a negotiator doesn't always require dramatic speeches or bravado. Sometimes all it takes is for you to remain calm. People often look to their leaders before looking at themselves. Calm is indeed contagious, and it goes beyond situations of crisis. It's also a negotiating tool. Calm creates a feeling of safety, the kind that paves the way for trust, safety and better communication. In the world of dealmaking, calm creates clarity while conveying confidence. All of this adds up to a favorable power dynamic.

The Time I was Tested: 4 Weeks to pull off the Impossible.

Overseeing the most important fitness showcase event in the world comes with its share of challenges. But nothing could have prepared me for what went down in the fall of 2020 when a global pandemic brought the world to its knees.

It typically takes about 8 months to produce Olympia Weekend. The event is a six day experience that includes a series of preliminary elements, highlighted by a significant stage production and a major trade show that covers more than a half a million square feet at the Las Vegas Convention Center. Event promotion, ticketing, sponsorships, exhibitor sales, budgeting, marketing, licensing, travel coordination, supply management, promotion, the list goes on – it's a massive undertaking. The event has been held each year since 1965 and it also serves as the world championship of the bodybuilding & fitness world. The Superbowl of the fitness industry.

With the world on lock-down, events from coast to coast were being cancelled, one after the next. Government leaders were limiting public gatherings to small groups. **And then the bomb dropped!!**

With less than 5 weeks to go, we were notified by Las Vegas city leaders that we wouldn't be allowed to have an audience. I'll never forget those words, it felt like the room was in slow motion. All I could think about was the 8 months of planning, the effort our team put in, the late nights and early mornings, the thousands of tickets already sold, and the best bodybuilders on the planet in the final stages of grueling and intense training.

Suddenly, our biggest fear became a reality. We were advised to cancel the event.

Emotionally drained, I picked up the phone to call Olympia owner Jake Wood to deliver the news. It wasn't a complete surprise, but the finality of it hit us like a ton of bricks. But even at this moment, we were calm. There was no panic. I said to Jake that I had a plan. He later confessed that he thought I was crazy. After all, it would be impossible to move the event to another city with only a few weeks to go. A total reset of something that normally requires 8 months of relentless preparation. A seemingly impossible task.

Event producers from around the world looked at us like we were crazy, and maybe we were. But we stayed calm, pulled the team together, and built a plan. I called it "Operation Impossible".

I'll spare you the details. That's a story for another day, another book. But in the end, we set our emotions aside. There was no panic. Just laser focused execution. And on December 16th, in Orlando, Florida, roughly 2,000 miles away from the Las Vegas Strip, amid strict COVID protocols, the 2020 Olympia was held. It was dubbed *The event that nearly never happened*. Thanks to Florida Governor Ron DeSantis, we were welcomed with open arms. Every seat was filled, champions were crowned, and more importantly than all of that, I discovered, beyond a shadow of a doubt, that the only limitations are the ones we place on ourselves. Especially if our mind is trained to be stronger than our feelings. Calm, cool, collected.

The Emotionally Impaired Leader

Let's talk about the alternative. What happens when leaders are emotionally fragile or reactive? Impulsive decisions, uncalculated, and full of blind spots. They let nostalgia override performance, they let personal relationships impede results, and they pay the price in time, money, and credibility.

It's incredibly difficult to reach the top of your field if your emotions drive your decisions. And that doesn't just apply to high-stakes deals. It applies to hiring, firing, investing, scaling, negotiating, even mentoring. <u>You must train your mind to run the show</u>.

Logic & Passion Can Co-Exist

Yes, the brain should have the final word, but the heart should *always* have a voice.

Why?

Because the heart is where passion lives. It's the origin of purpose. It's where instincts are born and it's the place from which you dream, create, and connect. The key is to not confuse *emotional noise* with *emotional truth*. They're not the same.

Be sure to know the difference between a gut instinct and a fear driven response. The most successful people use their heart to identify *what truly matters*, then they let their brain determine *how to pursue it*.

Situational Thinking vs Sentimental Thinking

Let's get tactical. Imagine this…You're considering promoting a team member. You *like* them. They've been loyal. But they lack the skills.

Do you:
A) Promote them because you *feel bad* not rewarding loyalty?
B) Choose the person who will best perform and grow the company?

Every day, leaders make costly sentimental decisions because they haven't trained their mind to override emotion with logic. Winning requires ruthless clarity. Not cruelty. Not coldness. Just clarity.

Emotional Maturity = Business Leverage

Emotional maturity is your ability to:

- Slow your response.
- Identify your triggers.
- Remain steady under fire.
- Act with long-term clarity, not short-term validation.

This is a superpower in business and in life. It makes you more credible, more persuasive, more respected, and best of all – more effective as a leader.

You can be inspiring and strategic. Compassionate and calculated. Empathetic and effective. To illustrate, let's take a look at two companies: Company A and Company B.

Company A: The leader of this company is highly analytical but has low emotional maturity. They make decisions based on data alone, frequently overlooking the emotional and relational aspects of their team. Over time, employee morale drops, productivity wanes, and innovative thinking dwindles.

Company B: This leader balances data-driven decisions with a high EQ. They actively listen to their team's ideas, acknowledge their emotional states, and create open communication for feedback. This leader is not only aware of their emotions but also adept at managing them, leading to a motivated, engaged, and innovative workforce.

Which company do you think has a better chance of weathering storms and achieving long-term success? The blend of emotional intelligence with strategic acumen becomes a formula for sustainable growth and resilience.

Self Mastery

You don't have to eliminate emotion. You just have to *elevate* your thinking above it. I call this self-mastery. And self-mastery precedes success.

Your reactions are rarely about the *thing* that happened. They're about past patterns, insecurities, ego or fear. The best leaders don't just *feel*, they *investigate* their feelings. They zoom out. They gain perspective. They disarm the emotional landmines before they blow up progress.

A Few Tactical Strategies

Want to train your mind to lead? Try these out:

1. **Create Pause**
   Before reacting, take a few seconds. Breathe. Ask: "What would the leader version of me do at this moment?"
2. **Pre-Plan Your Responses**
   Identify high-stakes scenarios and decide how you'll respond, *in advance.*

3. **Lead from Data, Not Drama**

   When emotions rise, revert to the numbers and the facts.

4. **Have a Mental Reset Routine**

   Step outside. Splash cold water. Call a mentor. Do something to shift energy before acting.

5. **Reframe Emotional Pain as Opportunity**

   Pain = information. What is it teaching you?

6. **Stay Physically Regulated**

   Your nervous system impacts your decision-making. Move. Breathe. Hydrate. Rest.

7. **Get Feedback from Mentors**

   Invite honest and open evaluation.

Let Your Brain Do its Thing

Emotions will always play a role in business, but the burden is on you to make sure logic prevails. Allow your logic and experience to protect you from the hazards of impulsive thinking and sentimental bullshit. The heart deserves a voice, but winning requires the BRAIN to have the final word.

Your heart matters. Your feelings matter. Your instincts matter. But they're not always right.

When the stakes are high, let your brain protect you. Let your mind translate your passion into big wins. Let your logic shield you from the fog of reactive behavior. Train yourself, daily, to pause, process, and power forward.

Because feelings are temporary, but your decisions are permanent.

So when emotions run high, ask yourself if you're reacting or responding. Let your heart guide your passion, but let your mind lead the way. That balance is the Winfuel that drives massive, sustainable success.

STAY CONNECTED!!!
YOUR WINFUEL JOURNEY
DOESN'T END HERE

ACCESS MORE WINFUEL * NEW CONTENT
* EVENTS * MERCHANDISE * COACHING

www.WINFUEL.com

ACKNOWLEDGEMENTS & GRATITUDE

For Grace. The best person I know. Beautiful in all the ways that matter...and even in the ways that don't.

To Dad, I wish you could've seen all of this. Your life taught me as much as your death.

To Mom, keep singing, keep laughing. You're one-of-a-kind.

To the rest of the world's smallest family, every story has a Chapter 1. Thanks for being mine.

To Jim Manion, your guidance, love and wisdom are gifts beyond measure. Tyler is ready.

To Jake Wood, if there was a PhD in loyalty, you would have it.

To Darrem Charles, where would I be without you?

To Big Steve, some friendships are just different.

To Robin & Dave, you've always known what's important.

To my entire Olympia family, the best of the best.

To Angelica Nebbia, my ride or die. To Sammy DaGrossa, my secret weapon.

To Lesley Visser, you taught us to cross when it said, "Don't Walk".

To the Real Ones, those who lift me up: Bill Kennedy, Jon Simon, Joe Kohn, Rob Wilkins, Adam Jablin, Sam Tejada, Mike Z, Nick Vespi, Mark Anthony, Mel Chancey, Tim Gardner, Nick Soto, Chef Rush, Charles Eggleston, Shaq, Roc & the DDM.

To my friends from the 305 all the way to the manicured streets of Parkland. If you know you know.

To the Baltimore Orioles, because it's so much more than a game.

To the elite champions who compete on our stages, keep inspiring.

To the millions who live the fitness lifestyle, never forget why you started.

To the men & women who serve & protect our country and our communities. Thank you.

To my personal Think Tank......You know who you are.

And finally, to my son Nicholas. Your capacity to learn is astounding, your ability to move through life, above it all, is a thing of beauty. There's nothing I'll ever do that'll make me prouder than being your dad. The world is yours.

The Olympia brings the global fitness industry together each year. This was our main stage production for the 60th Anniversary event held in Las Vegas (2024). The event is the subject of a new movie called DREAM BIG, now streaming on Amazon Prime Video.

It's always fun welcoming the biggest stars in the world. Celebrities like Mark Wahlberg help us build powerful bridges to new audiences.

For 25 years, Darrem Charles has held me accountable for every set and every rep. There is no greater investment than the one you make in yourself. I owe a lot to the trainer who became my brother.

What ever Dwayne Johnson touches turns to gold. He and I are both University of Miami guys and it's incredible to witness what happens the moment he enters a room.

Talkin' shop with the man who started it all. Joe Weider.

Imagine the excitement when ROCKY showed up at the Olympia. Thanks Sly!!

Everyone needs a "Jim Manion" in their life. I'm just glad I got the original.

Trying to convince Jimmy Fallon to book Mr. Olympia on the Tonight Show!!!

The city of Las Vegas and the fitness industry have enjoyed a win-win relationship for decades. It was a moment of triumph for all bodybuilding fans when the Olympia was presented with the Key to the Las Vegas Strip at a special ceremony during the summer of 2024.

We had ourselves a great cast for a movie I co-produced called BIGGER (2018). Julianne Hough played the role of Betty Weider. The movie tells the story of the men who pioneered an entire industry.

Back in my hosting days, I used to enjoy opportunities to interview some of the most inspiring people. Arnold and I don't always see eye to eye, but his impact on the world is incredible. Arnold is truly one of one.

Olympia owner Jake Wood and I pay close attention to what Dana White and his team have built in the world of MMA. The UFC has become a movement, an identity, and one of the most valuable brands in sports. Their story is loaded with lessons for all of us.

Everyone has a favorite place. This is ours. (Camden Yards, Baltimore)

My crew.

In Memory of

Joe & Ben Weider

Shawn Perine & Peter McGough

www.ingramcontent.com/pod-product-compliance
Lightning Source LLC
Chambersburg PA
CBHW041627140626
46547CB00031B/1119